266·3

MULTIPLYING CHURCHES IN MODERN INDIA

AN EXPERIMENT IN MADRAS

by

Shree M. EZRA SARGUNAM

Published by :

FEDERATION OF EVANGELICAL CHURCHES IN INDIA

First Edition — 1974

PRICE RS. 3

Copies can be had from :

ECI — LITERATURE DEPARTMENT
5, WADDELL ROAD — KILPAUK
MADRAS-600010 — INDIA

Printed at H.B.I. Press, Madras-600010

TO

MY GURUJI

Dr. DONALD A. McGAVRAN

FOREWORD

It is an exciting experience these days to travel and to meet all sorts of potential young people in India's struggling church. Their names are not widely known; at least, not yet. But in the next decade or so some of them will make a name, for their life, ministry and contribution to the extension of God's Kingdom will be gradually and effectively felt. In fact there are evidences that they are here as God's instruments for this generation in India.

One such young man is the Rev. M. Ezra Sargunam of the Evangelical Church of India founded by the OMS International. At present he is the Chairman and District Superintendent of the Madras area. He is one of those dynamic young men who have a vision and a burden for the extension of God's Kingdom in India.

His book is immensely interesting because it has a personal flavour, and yet it is not so subjective, because his whole desire is to present a case objectively. In this he has a powerful argument, for it is authentic and based on actual experiments and experiences in the establishment and the growth of the Evangelical Church of India, especially in the Madras area. He gives historical perspective when necessary and a personal touch when appropriate. As a true son of the soil, he is passionately concerned for the depressed classes. He is keenly aware of the cultural and the political ferment particularly in Tamilnadu, and takes the opportunity to apply church growth principles in such situations.

If he is at times too frank and candid in his statements, we can understand; for he is in real earnest to get going. He is not a mere theorist; he is right there in the midst of action, taking a leading part in one of the fastest growing churches in one section of India. There is no reason why this experiment cannot be multiplied all over India to see much church growth in this needy land.

I commend to all the reading of his **Multiplying Churches in Modern India.** May this provide impetus and inspiration to all in the church to join hands in a great and challenging enterprise—to transform India's area of darkness into a kingdom of love and light.

New Delhi,
June 29, 1974.

I. BEN WATI
Evangelical Fellowship of India.

PREFACE

This book in its original form was submitted by me to the Fuller Theological Seminary as a thesis entitled, "Multiplying Churches in Urban India — An experiment in Madras" in partial fulfilment of the requirements for the Degree of M.A. in Missiology in May 1973. Since then the thesis has undergone considerable improvement to bring it into this present book form.

I am grateful to the "Lord of the Harvest" for giving me the opportunity to pursue my study and research in the School of World Missions. I definitely see the guidance of God, because this privilege came exactly in time when we were making hard, bold plans to multiply churches in Madras and in other parts of India.

I am greatly indebted to my Guruji Dr. Donald McGavran under whose personal guidance I have been able to carry on this research. He spared no pains in shaping my thinking and counselling with me during our weekly research seminar.

I want to thank the Fuller Theological Seminary for granting me a research fellowship and for my Mission, OMS International, in meeting the balance of expense involved in this study programme.

I heartily thank all my pastor colleagues especially Rev. P. J. Sadhu Singh, lay leaders, friends and missionaries in Madras and Dr. David J. Rigby of the Lebanon Bible College, England for their help and co-operation in this research. Words cannot be found to express my deep appreciation to Rev. and Mrs. Houghton, our present missionaries and co-labourers in the ministry, for encouraging me to carry on my studies as well as to publish this book. I also record my gratitude to the Houghtons for many valuable suggestions they have made and for the proof reading of the manuscript.

I am grateful to Dr. I. Ben Wati for graciously reading the manuscript and contributing the Foreword.

My special thanks are due to Mrs. Sally Vinson of Whittier, California, for undertaking to type the rough draft and final copy free of charge. Most of all I am thankful to Mr. D. K. Arulnesan, Manager of the H.B.I. Press, and his staff, for the excellent job he has done to get this book printed in time.

May the pages of this book be a source of inspiration to such readers who are sent by the "Lord of the Harvest" as labourers into the Indian fields which are white and ready for the harvest.

5, Waddell Road
MADRAS-600010
INDIA

M. EZRA SARGUNAM

TABLE OF CONTENTS

(i)

INTRODUCTION

India has always been a mystery to the world outside. The Greek historian Herodotus wrote about India's glittering gold. Perhaps, this caught the imagination of Alexander the Great and made him march eastward. To Marco Polo, the splendor and beauty of the Court of Genghis Kahn of China was nothing compared to the wealth of South India. Several centuries later, Vasco da Gama, the Portuguese traveller landed on the western shores of India, while Columbus, who set out to arrive at the eastern coast of India by traveling westward, finally arrived on the shores of America. Also came the Moguls, the Portuguese, the French and the British. So they all came seeking the "riches" of India. The search goes on. Thousands of bewildered youths from the materialistic west are rushing here today wondering whether India has the answer to their spiritual problems.

This land of mystery, and this land of myth, after several hundred years of foreign domination is now an independent and free nation. India is today an awakening giant. Since Independence, fighting against odds, [overcoming obstacles, the country has achieved tremendous progress in many fields. The British linked every part of the country with the railways and this brought about a great mobility within the country. The architects of new India laid great stress on industries. This and several other causes, with which I will be dealing in this book, are the determining factors which are moving the country rapidly toward urbanization. Only 20 per cent of the Indian population live in cities, but the "urban mood" is strongly felt in remote parts of the new India. Consequently, though my entire research is focused on the city of Madras and the newly planted churches of the Evangelical Church of India, I am confident that my findings will be of general interest among those who are deeply involved with evangelism and missions in any part of the country, for that matter, any part of the world.

In these days when we stand at a crossroads in missions, the need to evangelize and multiply churches in modern cities is urgent. To a certain extent, the crisis in missions today is due to our inability to multiply churches in the ever-growing modern cities. If we fail to disciple the urban population, take it for certain, we will fail to disciple the rural population too. If we fail to capture the cities for Christ, it goes without saying, we will lose the villages, too. If the new settler in the city with his new outlook and openness does not respond to the Gospel as we voice it, the villager with his fixed and frozen state of mind, is not going to make a positive commitment to the Christian faith.

I said it is urgent to plant churches in the urban areas these days because of the rapidity with which the country is being urbanized and the main line Churches in India seem to be little concerned about discipling city populations. The cities are and have always been strategic points for trade, politics, government, and the expansion of all sects of all creeds. From the standpoint of discipling peoples, cities are beyond doubt strategic points. Strong and well nourished city churches can become the means of church growth in the whole country round about. This was what happened with St. Paul's ministry in the Roman provinces of Asia. The Gospel spread from the cities to the countryside—and this is exactly what is happening in Madras.

So then, the purpose of my book is to affirm that Christians can today multiply sound churches in Asian cities by purposive action based on biblical principles. I shall illustrate my thesis by the twenty-year efforts of the OMS International in planting churches in Madras city, which resulted in the birth of the Evangelical Church of India (hereafter called ECI), a small, rapidly growing denomination consisting of 35 congregations, with about 2,500 full members, and a community of 5,000. (ECI congregations in other parts of India number about fifteen, but this book does not take them into account.

As necessary background to this study, I am tracing the culture and language of the Tamil people, urbanization in modern India as illustrated from Madras, and a brief description of other denominations in the city.

2

In the major sections of the book, I will describe in detail the evolution of "The Madras Plan" used by the OMS International (hereafter simply called the OMS). I have given the English equivalents of the Hindi and Tamil terms when I used them. Here and there I use the symbols C^1, C^2, and C^3 to indicate conversions from non-Christians, nominal Christians of other denominations, and Conversions from our own ECI families, respectively.

Parts of this book have a personal flavor. On occasion, like the author of Acts, I break over into the use of "we" and "our." My experience of the Christian life and of the evangelization of urban communities colors them. My commitment to the cause of the Dravidian movement and Dravidian Christians shines through here and there. Yet, I trust that what I say is true. It has been my constant concern to state the facts and to describe exactly what occurred.

I was born to God-fearing, born-again parents in a remote village in the southern tip of Tamilnadu. My father was a great man of prayer. On July 19, 1938, several hours before I was to be born, my father opened his Bible to have his early morning devotion. As he opened the Bible, the Book of Ezra came before him. He then turned to read the portion of the day, which happened to be Nehemiah, Chapter 8. Even in this chapter, the name Ezra was mentioned about nine times, relating all that God had done through him. It became evident to my father that the Lord was going to bless his family with a boy child and that he should give him this name and dedicate him for the ministry of God. That is how I happened to get my name. But, it was not until 1954, at the age of sixteen that I accepted Christ.

In July of the same year, I joined the Madras Bible Seminary, finding myself to be the smallest and the most dejected among all the other students. The minimum age requirement for a person to be enrolled in the seminary was eighteen. But by God's divine providence and plan. I managed to get into the seminary at the age of sixteen! Let me quote recollections of Rev. G. Phillippe, who was the Principal of the seminary then

During the intervening years we have followed the
growth of the work in the Madras area with

3

great interest, and we have thought again and again of the question, 'Who hath despised the day of small things ?' Speaking of small things reminds us of the day Ezra Sargunam arrived at 5 Waddell Road. He was such a small thing, and looked so young, we were about to send him back home immediately. He pleaded to remain to the end of the probation period. By that time he had so established a personal record in conduct, as well as academically we let him stay. (Phillippe, Personal Memoir, 3).

But the problem was not over. I was undergoing severe personal and spiritual struggles. I was doing all right in the classroom, but was a great failure in the fieldwork. On one occasion I had to pay a fine for not having taken a preaching turn in a student camp. I shall never forget how Dr. and Mrs. Rigby took special pains to shape me up in those days. After my graduation, I served one year as an assistant to several pastors here and there. In July, 1958, I was asked to move to a suburban village called Porur where I was given a last chance to prove myself. Perhaps I accepted the appointment as there was no other alternative.

We began laboring in the area. I was unable to lead the seminary students as they came on the week-ends to help me. Several weeks rolled on and I began to discover that 90 per cent of the village population couldn't read and write. This faced me with a challenge and I began taking adult literacy classes. Many young men and adults took great interest. We followed the Laubach method. I began to gain confidence because at last I had found a group of young Harijans who had respect for me and began to look at me as their leader. I made a determined effort to lead these young men into the Christian experience. Months passed by nothing remarkable happened among these men of Porur village.

One night after twelve o'clock, I suddenly woke up from my sleep because there was such noise and fanfare out on the streets It was an annual festival night for the local deity worshipped in

4

the village. As I stood by the window, I saw the men bringing their goddess in a decorated chariot amidst great music, singing, and dancing, From among the crowd, I saw some of those boys who were attending my night classes. I stood by the window with tears flooding my eyes as the light from the passing procession came through the window and fell on my face. That was the first occasion in which I was moved by the Holy Spirit with compassion for the people who are lost in the world to paganism. From that day on I was a different person. I set to work before God to bring about a change in the lives of those young Hindus. The Lord began to work miracles. The following year during the festival night, all those boys stayed with me in my home and we had an all-night prayer meeting.

This kind of personal experience, the constant vision for the perishing and the consuming burden for the lost is characterized in the lives and ministry of my colleagues and most of the believers of our congregations. I bear witness to this fact throughout the book.

I would like to make just one other clarification as to my position regarding "caste." I am fully aware that caste is a dirty word in India. However, readers may find that I freely use it for purely academic reasons. More than that, in my research, I have confirmed my previous estimates that the *Harijans* are the most responsive community in India. In order to be an effective servant of the Master and to fully identify myself with this community I have determined to become a Harijan, renouncing my previous "caste status" which is "claimed to be" higher. This decision I have taken after clear guidance from God. Hence, naturally readers will find me favoring this particular community to which I and my family now belong.

This book must be understood as written by the man who has experienced these things. From chapter to chapter— more in some than others—its subjective quality will come through. Readers may kindly make allowances for it, observing however that it is interwoven with a tough-minded objective discussion of urban evangelization. Indeed, an objective view of urban evangelization in India dominates great sections of the book, which throughout is based on facts. For example, I

5

have stated the methods, policies, and principles adopted by the OMS International etablishing indigenous churches. I have mentioned the missiological factors which were chief causes for the church growth we experienced in Madras. I have made certain proposals and recommendations for an urban strategy which might be followed by other denominations. I have also proposed an overall strategy to disciple the responsive populations of India.

CHAPTER I—TAMILIANS OF MADRAS

One cannot very well say anything about a movement, however small it might be, without making some mention about the land and the people. In this opening chapter, I shall attempt to give a brief description of the early culture of the Tamil people, tracing it to the present. It was within this culture that Christianity took root in the last half of the first century, and it was among this ancient people that the OMS International was called to evangelize and multiply strong, evangelical churches in the last half of this century.

A. INDIA AND TAMILNADU

India is the largest democratic country in the world of today with a population of 548 million people (547, 949, 809), of which there are, under the category of Scheduled Castes and Scheduled Tribes, 117 million :(79,995,896 ÷ 38,015,162). The southernmost state of India, Tamilnadu, in which urban church planting is taking place, has a population of 41,199,168, of which the Scheduled Castes number 7,315,595 and Scheduled Tribe 311,515 (Census of India, 1971).

The two major races, the Dravidian and Aryan have mingled very much with each other down through the centuries. Yet, in India, south of the Vindhya Mountains (see Fig. 1) the Dravidians easily outnumber the Aryans. The State of Tamilnadu. for which Madras is the capital, has been very sensitive to "Dravidian feelings."

If there has been more response in the past to Christianity in the South than in the North, it is partly because of the liberation my people, the Tamilians, have found in Christianity after many centuries of Aryan-Brahmin suppression.

I shall set forth in the rest of this chapter the origin of the Dravidians, their degradation, and their more recent revolt against Brahminism in the State of Tamilnadu. The study of Tamilians means the study of Dravidians, as the Dravidians are the Tamilians. At the same time, the Dravidian race also includes the present Malayalam—, Telugu—, and Kananese-speaking populations in the Deccan Plateau.

7

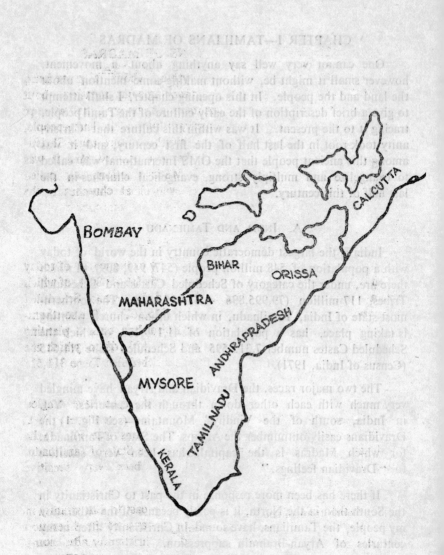

FIG. 1 : Map showing the portion of India wherein the Dravidian population is in excess of Aryan.

B. The Dravidian and Aryan Races

Historians, anthropologists, and philologists agree that the Dravidians are the original inhabitants of India. But where did they come from ?

1. The Origin of the Dravidians :

Some hold that the Dravidians have been in South India since the remotest ages. A little over the hundred years ago, in 1856, Bishop Robert Caldwell presented his theory of their link with peoples outside of India. The linguistic evidence, as he saw it, suggested affinities with Scythian languages and particularly Finno-Ugric branch. This view had earlier been espoused by Rask and Muller, but Caldwell was the first to state the theory in a systematic fashion.

Since Caldwell, several other scholars have taken his approach that Dravidians came from Mid-Asia much earlier than the Aryans. Dr. N. Lahovary in his book on *Dravinian Origins and the West* quotes Prof. Chatterji as saying :

> Anthropologists assume at least three varieties or modifications of the Mediterranean races having come to India, and all of these would appear to have been speakers of Dravidian.
>
> (1963 : 35)

Caldwell also pointed to the influence of the Dravidian languages upon Sanskrit and assumed that Dravidian speakers, therefore, must at one time have inhabited much of India—the North as well as the South. In addition, he speculated concerning their physical type and their cultural connections. He considered the Dravidians to be basically caucasoid, and he referred to existence of megalithic monuments in South India and close similarity of these to the megaliths of Western Europe.

> (1856 : 508-524)

Since the first appearance of Caldwell's epochal work, numerous scholars have addressed themselves to the problem of the origin and early development of the entity we call "Dravidian." A number of archaeological discoveries, particularly that of Indus Valley (Mohanijadaro. Harappa Civilizations) assume that the language spoken there was an early from of Dravidian.

There is yet another theory that the Dravidians have had a southern origin. The hypothetical, sunken continent in the Indian Ocean, called Lemuria, is thought to have been their original home. (Cooke 1897 : 198) Ceylon is certainly Dravidian, and the distribution of Dravidians in India lends itself as well to the support of a southern origin as of a northern one.

Bishop Caldwell's theory on the supposed affinity of the Dravidian race to the Sctyhian race has not been fully accepted. However :

> Caldwell's linguistic theory has not been success-
> fully supplanted by any other, and in fact it
> has recently become a topic of renewed interest
> for a number of scholars. (Sjoberg 1971 : 3).

Gleason's *Introduction to Descriptive Linguistics* says, "of all such proposals [and theories] the best that can be said is that they are not proven." (479)

While there may be difference of opinion as to the origin of Dravidian race, there is no question whatsoever that when the Aryan invaders came to India, they found another race in posses sion of the land—a race they gradually subjugated and to some extent assimilated.

2. The Aryan-Dravidian "Rift"

It is interesting to observe the reaction of the Aryans against their predecessors. The hymns of the Rig Veda give us much light on the long struggle of the Aryans in conquering the Dravidians. The Aryans were not lacking in epithets with which to describe these people. They called them "enemies," "slaves," "abject tribes," "void of sense," "inhuman," "keeping alien rites," "malignant," "wicked,", "riteless," "prayerless" "bestowing no gifts" (to the gods), "pouring no oblation of milk' "non-worshippers," "priestless," "not keeping: the fires," "worshipper of mad gods," and they even accused them of eating human flesh. (Bessey 1915 : 10).

This is an exaggerated description; for the conquerors speak also of their enemies being wealthy in herds, having impregnable castles, forts of iron and cities. (Ibid,) But how such a unique and civilized people step-by-step surrendered themselves to the

Aryans is a matter that would intrigue anyone. Further, however civilized the Dravidians might have been, their great failure was that they kept no records of their deep and profound belief system. In this, the Aryans seemed to have had the advantage over the Dravidians.

> If we assume that some Dravidian speakers at last, perhaps three and a half to four millennia ago, formed part of the Harappa civilization, with its cities and its special script the question arises: why is there no record of non-Aryan writing system in South India? Writing so far as we know, was an Aryan introduction.
>
> (Sjoberg 1971 : 7)

This may not be altogether a correct judgment, as there are enough evidences to ancient Tamil literature as old, and sometimes much older than the Sanscrit literature.

The Dravidians, however militant they might have been, were overcome by the Aryans and thereupon, perhaps, moved to the South. Even there, the Brahmins did not leave them alone. They followed them. There is hypothesis that, as the Dravidians moved to the South, they met and by stages mingled with some type of primitive people who might have been there already before them.

3. The Caste System

The caste system was originally confined to the abode of Aryans namely-*Aryavarta* (from Himalayan Mountains to the Vindhya Mountain between North and South and from the Arabian sea to the Bay of Bengal between East and West).

The Dravidians were a race without caste. The great Tamil poet, Valluvar of the first century writes as if there were no caste. It is probably against this casteless society that some Aryan Brahminical writings are directed.

> Those countries are called barbarous (*mleksha*) where the system of four castes does not exist; the other are denoted *Aryavarta* (the abode of Aryan). (Sacred Books of the East 1895: Vol. 2, 34).

11

Gradually, however, as the Brahmin conquest pressed South, the Dravidians succumbed to the evil system of caste. In the course of time the conquest was complete. The Aryans (Brahmins) became the high caste and forced the Dravidians to take a subordinate position in the newly-organized caste system.

In the Vedas, caste means color (*varna*) and the caste system is known as "*Varnashra Dharma.*" It is believed that the caste system, whether in North or South, has been partly determined by the color of the skin, as the "superior" Aryans were light in color and the "inferior" Dravidians were dark. It is usually understood that of four castes of Hiduism, the *Sudras* only are Dravidians, but it is likely that very few people in India (South or North) who claim descent from the *Vaisysas* end *Kshatrias* are of pure Aryan origin. (Thurston 1908 : Vol. IV, 79; Vol. VII, 271). For instance, Thurston points out the *Komaties*, or merchants, who claim to be *Vaisysas* appear to have intimate connection with the *Madigas* who are undoubtedly of Dravidian origin. When a marriage takes place among the Komaties, it is necessary to bring the fire from the house of a Madiga for the new household. Many devices are used to cover up this connection. A Komatie will come on some pretext to the house of Madiga, and after completing business will ask for a light for his *cheroot* (cigar). Komaties, however, do not deny the connection.

(Ibid., Vol. III, 325)

This is just one of the hundreds of cases in which the legends tell us how one caste claimed superiority to the other. The early literature in the Tamil language bears witness to the fact that there were four different classes of peeple :

"*Anthanar*" - Priests (mostly referred to as celibates)

"*Arasar*" - Kings

"*Vanigar*" - Merchants

"*Vellalar*" - Farmers

While these four belonged to the "high order," there was yet one other class of people of a "low order," whose duty it was to do the menial jobs. (Phillai 1935 : 79–89) So here, among the Tamils who once had no caste, we have the castes and the outcaste pattern the Aryans introduced.

12

Indeed in Tamilnadu, the caste system has been more oppressive and complicated than in North India, since the Mogul invasion has not affected the South much. The Brahmins comprise less than 3 per cent of the population, while the Dravidians (probably not all of them pure Dravidians) comprise the rest.

In the city of Madras and the suburbs and in the villages of Tamilnadu where our ministry is now extended, our church planting has been found to be effective mostly among two Dravidian castes, namely the *Harijans* and the *Nadars*, The Harijan (people of God) who were once known as "outcastes" under the Hindu caste system, are a remarkable, hard-working people and our C[1] conversions are mostly from among them.

This ethnic group among whom we have had spectacular success in planting churches used to be called *Parayans*, and for centuries were the most suppressed class of people in South India. Thurston in *Castes and Tribes in South India*, has an extensive article on Parayan, in which he says that they acknowledge the existence of a supreme, omnipresent, personal, spiritual being, the source of all they call "*Kadavul*" (He who is). This Tamil word also has the meaning " He who transcends man's mind and spirit." "Kadavul" possesses no temples and is not worshipped. Thurston, therefore, thinks that the priests of this community represent a very ancient order and that the whole community is very ancient. Ten centuries ago they were in respectable circumstances and that many were weavers. N. C. Sargant, making comment about this community says :

> It is indeed difficult to account for the gradual
> degradation and economic enslavement of such
> people. Yet at the same time one wonders
> whether such a heritage of better things in the
> past may offer an explanation for the amazing
> ability of such Tamil people to rise above the
> disadvantages of their former economic and
> social position. The Christian religion in
> bringing them deliverance from bondage of fear
> and evil spirits, has also called back to their

13

> consciousness ideas and ideals entombed in
> their language. The Christian message of sin
> and salvation, when heard. is welcomed as true
> by the thoughtful Tamilians, and has indeed
> brought freedom from the bondage of evil
> spirits and bad habits, from degradation and
> destitution. (1962 : 4)

These are some of the factors which made the Tamilians, particularly the Harijans, respond readily to the message of Christ which liberates the suppressed masses.

I will be dealing with the subject of the Christian approach to caste in the last chapter.

4. The Religion of the Dravidians
   Caldwell says :

> They [the Tamilians] were without hereditary
> 'priests' and idols, and appear to have had
> no idea of 'heaven' or 'hell,' of the
> 'soul' or 'sin' ; but they acknowledged the
> existence of God, whom they styled 'ko'
> (or King)—a realistic title little known to
> Orthodox Hinduism. They erected to his
> honor a temple which they called koil 'God's
> house' ; but I cannot find any trace of
> 'worship' which they offered to him.
> (Encyclopedia of Religion and Ethics 1935 :
> Vol. 3, 1)

At the same time, Caldwell also feels that the basic beliefs of the South Indian Dravidian tribes should be called shamanism, while the North Indian Dravidian religion (sun and moon worship) should be called animism. Like followers of many indigenous religions, the dravidians worshipped the "Earth-Mother". This, in later ages, developed into a general Mother Cult, which together with the worship of *Kali*, the black and blood-thirsty goddess, and *Devi* and *Kumari* (as in *Kanya Kumari*) and virgin deities, were imported into Hinduism.

14

The Aryans found that if they were to hold the Dravidians in subjection, some consideration for their religion was necessary. Although the Dravidians were, according to the earliest Aryans, worshippers of "mad gods" they were most tenacious of their religious rites. The Aryans did not attempt to compel them to give up their gods, but adopted the policy of bringing the people with their religion into the fold of a religion, later to be known as Hinduism. Thus, Aryan religion made enormous changes in the direction of Dravidian religion. For instance, the worship of *Siva* is Dravidian in origin. In the worship of Siva, there is a great deal that is opposed to Brahminism.

Siva, his wife *Parvathi*, who appears in many forms like *Kali* and *Durga*, *Ganesa*, the elephant-headed god, and *Hanuman*, the monkey god who are said to be the sons of Siva, are all supposed to be gods of Dravidian origin (perhaps during some later period) but are now firmly parts of the Hindu pantheon. The original Vedic religion finds but little in common with modern Hinduism.

What is Hinduism ? No one will ever be able to answer that question. Who are the Hindus ? No one can ever even know that for sure. The *Jana Sangh* party's leader Vijapay thinks that all those who live in India are Hindus (Ram 1968 : 22) Brahminism or Hinduism, whatever one might call this religious system, has for more than 3000 years excluded the depressed castes. They were not "Hindus" They lived outside the villages and they had their own gods.

The census takers always had difficulty discovering who were and who were not Hindus. I quote here a few passages from the census book which indicates the kind of problems the British Government had to face over this issue back in 1911.

> It is well to remember that the strict connotation
> of the word Hinduism is racial and social
> rather than theological. At the same time we
> may admit that Hinduism is in a sense acquisi-
> tive. If it strains out the individual gnat, it
> can swallow with cheerfulness the tribal camel,
> Some slight profession of faith, and modern

15

efficiency in the nice conduct of ceremony, are sufficient to secure for an aspiring animistic tribe, gods included, admission within the pale.

The most debatable Hindu may well worship, and often does worship, the great Hindu deities. Such worship is not a necessary impediment to a simultaneous worship of many minor godlings. The two acts of faith at times co-exist even in Brahmins.

Whatever may be their present-day union or interminglement, it is difficult to imagine any original connection of the Aryan Brahmins and their subtle philosophies, with the gross demonolatry of the Dravidian peoples who surrounded them. Holding certain philosophical opinions, which they neither expected nor particularly desired their Dravidian neighbours to share, it is unlikely that the early Aryan theorists made any serious efforts to obtain adherents to their way of thinking. But satisfied with the admission of their undoubted intellectual superiority, they built gradually many a connecting bridge between their own somewhat unpractical speculations, and the extremely materialistic demonologies of the Dravidians.

E. A. Gait, Census Commissioner for India, in his ' Notes on Census Returns of Hindus ', dated Simla, 12th July, 1910 (see *Indian Social Reformer*, Bombay Nov. 20, 1912), discusses at length the question as to who are to be enumerated as Hindus. ' The complaint has often been made that the Census returns of Hindus are misleading, as they include millions of people who are not really Hindus at all, who are denied the ministrations of the Brahmins, and are forbidden to enter Hindu temples, and who in many cases are regarded as so unclean that their touch, or even their proximity causes pollution. There is of course much truth in the criticism, but the fact that Hinduism has no definite creed makes it difficult to lay down any definite test as to who is, and who is not a Hindu. A man may believe in the whole Hindu pantheon, or only in particular gods, or, for that matter, in no gods at all ; he may sacrifice or abstain from sacrifices ; he may eat flesh or abstain from so doing ; but he is still regarded as a Hindu if he belongs to a recognized Hindu caste, does not deny the supremacy of the Brahmins, and abstains from open disregard of the restrictions observed by his caste fellows.' Mr. Gait proposes the following as some of the tests which might be applied to discover whether any certain class may be regarded as Hindus or not. '(1) Do the members of the caste or tribe worship the great Hindu gods ? (2) Are they allowed to enter Hindu temples or make offerings at the shrine ? (3) Will good Brahmins act as their priests ? (4) Will degraded Brahmins do so? In that case, are they recognized as Brahmins by persons outside the caste, or are they Brahmins only in name? (5) Will clean castes take water from them ? (6) Do they cause pollution, (a) by touch, (b) by proximity?' These tests would cut off from Hlnduism all the outcastes, who are a very considerable number in the census, and who commonly claim to be genuine Hindus. (Census of 1911, Vol. XII, Pt. I, Ch. 4, paras. 4, 6, 22, 26).

However, about 1920, it became clear that Indians were going to be given the vote and the seventy million "untouchables" (non-Hindus) might vote as a separate block. It also became clear that these millions might opt for Christianity or team up

17

with the Muslims to form a majority thus ending the century-long Brahmin rule. Consequently, Brahmins with Mahatma Gandhi began announcing that the untouchables were really God's people (Harijans) and were "beloved Hindus" and gave them all sorts of concessions to hold them in line. This deceit-full policy did not commend itself to the anti-Brahmin Tamilians.

These are some of the factors that church planters in India must bear in mind. There is still a vast gap between the masses and Brahmin-ridden upper castes. Christ's way to India's heart, as Bishop Picket calls to our attention, is through the suppressed masses.

From one point of view there is no religion called Hinduism, no such religion exists. It is a waste of time to try and make Christianity " a crown of Hinduism ". The Christian should identify himself with the masses. The Brahminic religion is being shaken to the very root. The subtle Brahmins are not going to rule India any more. These are the days of the masses. I shall show in the rest of the chapter how the foundation to such a movement has already been laid in Tamilnadu among the Tamilians.

C. ANTI-BRAHMIN MOVEMENTS IN TAMILNADU.

The Christian religion is being propagated in the midst of this tremendous battle between Tamilians and the Hindu religion which has forced them into the caste system. Consequently, the anti-Hindu and anti-Brahmin movements of South India are of the greatest importance to urban evangelism and I turn to describe them here.

Perhaps the first somewhat successfull anti-Brahmin movement was led at least 600 years before Christ by no less than Gautama Buddha himself. Buddha questioned the validity of one becoming a Brahmin priest by heredity. He taught that no one is born into a caste. Instead, one's caste is decided by the deeds of the present and not the actions of past life.

One became *Sramana* (supreme) by equanimity, a Brahmin by chastity, a *Muni* by knowledge and a *Thapasa* (devotee) by penance...By one's

18

action he becomes a Brahmin, Kshatriya, or Vaishya, or Sudra. (Sacred Books of the East 1895 : Vol. 45, 140)

The weakness in Buddha's approach was that though he taught that anyone can become a Brahmin, he did not question the superiority of the Brahmin. He didn't choose to become a Sudra. He did not feel proud of being one. Instead he only aroused and created a new interest in the minds of the people and showed them the possibility of them also becoming Brahmins. Thereby, people only craved to become Brahmins. The order had not been changed. The superiority of the Brahmins had not been disturbed.

In a battle against the "Buddhist heresy" the Brahmins brought out laws calling on kings to punish all those Sudras attempting to assume the superior role of the twice born. (Law of Manu, Sacred Books of the East, 1895 : Vol. 25, 388) Ultimately Buddhism was completely wiped out in India.

Then for centuries the Brahmins and Brahminism went unchecked. Even during Mogul and British times the Brahmins occupied high positions and controlled the governments. Only after successful missionary activity and the conversion of millions of "untouchable" Sudras, and some tribesmen, the Brahmins became alarmed. For the first time Brahmins began identifying themselvs with the rest of the people of India and strong sentimental feelings were raised. G. Subramanya Iyer who helped to found the Indian National Congress and was the proprietor of The Hindu (a newspaper) in an editorial in December 18, 1895, stated that there was no point in "launching into tirades against the missionaries if we are not prepared to do something for ourselves." He asked :

Where are the Hindu schools and colleges, where are the orphanages and widow homes ? We think we have reached a stage when we must make a strong effort to depend on our own exertions. (Symposium on Dravidian Civiliza-tion 1971 : 150)

19

It is strange that the Brahmins like Subramanya Iyer began to talk as if they were really a part of the Dravidian masses. "We," "ourselves." "our own." These phrases are not natural to Brahmins. Brahmins were using them simply to hold the Dravidians in line, simply to keep them from leaving the Brahmin party.

But the Brahmin strategy met with stiff opposition in every field. C. Sankaran Nair and others even attacked Hinduism which—they asserted—is based upon the will and opinion of the Brahmins. They charged that it was the Brahmins who had created caste distinctions so characteristic of Hinduism.

D. DRAVIDA KAZHAGAM (THE DRAVIDIAN PARTY)

The much stronger anti-Brahmin feeling, coupled with centuries old antagonism against Aryan cultural imperialism on one hand and Brahmin domination in the political arena on the other emerged in the early twenties in Tamilnadu quite spontaneously under the charismatic leadership of E. V. Ramasami Naicker.

Ramasami Naicker did not have any school education after the age of ten. In 1904, as a young bridegroom of twenty-five, he went to the holy city of Benares. The city, he discovered, was no holier than any other. The Brahmins there ate meat and drank toddy and prostitution was a brisk business. (Irschick 1969-332) A change of attitude toward the Hindu religion and an anti-Brahmin feeling was born in his heart.

Later on he became a member of the Congress Party and advocated the removal of untouchability. Frustrated by Brahmin control in the Congress, he left it and joined the Justice Party. Later he founded the Dravida Kazhagam, a social reform movement. While the slogan demanding that the British quit India rent the air, the followers of EVR also demanded that the Aryan-Brahmins quit India along with the Britishers. The anti-Brahmin movement which began in 1920, gained momentum and became very militant in 1927, and the years following when the "Untoubles" and Sudras went marching into the streets of the Brahmin localities. On several occasions Brahmins were manhandled and

20

great terror prevailed throughout Tamilnadu. Brahmins began to reap all they had sowed for centuries. The DK actually demanded that Tamilnadu secede from India.

EVR and his followers went all over South India preaching to the masses that the early Dravidians were the most sophisticated race and that the Aryans with their vices and guile had distorted the truth and made the Dravidians appear to be "primitives." The DK men sharply criticized superstition and idol worship and smashed many idols. They exposed the Brahmin's subtle ideas which had influenced and infiltrated South Indian society through the Puranas. The gods and goddesses came under fire. For instance, one pamphlet, typical of many which were published, was entitled, *"Visitira Tevarkal Kottu"* (Wonderful Court of Deities). All the gods of the Hindu pantheon were subjected to a court of law for a severe cross-examination which showed up all the sexual and violent crimes they had committed. The gods, Shiva and Vishnu, and many lesser godlings were "convicted" and given harsh sentences. (Irschick, 1969:346)

In this way, the entire basis of Puranic Hinduism was questioned. Religion itself was attacked. It became the order of the day for youth to style themselves as non-religious revolutionary zealots.

A Self-Respect League was formed through which religious reforms took place. The Hindu marriages which for long had been conducted by Brahmin Priests were now conducted by the leaders of the Self-Respect League. Mr. P. Subarayan, a "self-respect" man became the Chief Minister of Madras as early as 1930, during the British rule.

Among the men who were trained in the school of EVR was a very prominent young man named C. N. Annadurai. Annadurai was a man of sohpistication and undoubted ability and EVR granted him an increasingly important role in the decisions of the Self-Respect Movement.

21

E. THE DRAVIDA MUNNETRA KAZHAGAM (DRAVIDIAN FORWARD PARTY)

Dravidian feelings found expression first in the Dravida Kazhagam (DK) and later in Dravida Munnetra Kazhakam (DMK), a political offshoot under the leadership of C. N. Annadurai who separated from the DK for personal reasons. DMK spread its ideas more vigorously among the masses than DK did and during the 1967 election captured the Madras State Assembly, which it renamed Tamilnadu. Ever since it came to power it has step by step put the Brahmins out of jobs and replaced them with non-Brahmins. "It is not too much to say that at the present time, the non-Brahmins in the Tamil area amply fulfill their role as lords of the soil and inheritors of noble traditions." (Irschick 1969:166).

Since their reelection in 1971 the DMK Government has also boldly utilized the temple properties and assets toward education and uplift of the poor. They have totally refused to accept Hindi as the national language of India. Uulike the DK the DMK attempted to build an image for themselves as non-atheists holding on to the most popular "One God One People" dictum of the Tamilians. (Ramanujam 1972:80)

I have written as if Hinduism and the worship of the Hindu pantheon had suddenly ceased to exist in Tamilnadu. This is of course a great oversimplification. Hinduism, the worship of the Hindu gods, the business of the great temples, the popular Hinduism of the villages, the fear of evil spirits, the worship of household deities, the sacrifice of coconuts and chickens, goats and flowers continues on with great force. And despite all the fulminations of the DMK about caste, the great objection to becoming Christian is that doing so ruins one's caste, breaks up one's family, leads one to join the "caste" of the Christians, or requires that one becomes "low caste."

In this chapter I have therefore overdrawn a picture in order to say that, because of the DMK revolt against Brahmin oppression which marks all the decades of this century since 1920, and will continue to mark them, the Gospel of Jesus Christ with its strong emphasis on justice and brotherhood has a notable opportunity to be heard. More people in Tamilnadu can *hear* the Gospel today than any other time in history. More people can *believe* Jesus Christ. Literally millions can entertain the idea that for Tamilians, Jesus (rather than the Hindu gods) is the Way, the Truth, and the Life. These are days to advance. Cowering down in our churches, seeking to avoid attention, keeping quiet about the Gospel, soft pedalling evangelism, going in heavily for social service, and talking ambiguously about "Union" and the social gospel are not what the hour demands. The hour demands renewed proclamation of Jesus Christ as the Liberator, the Way of Salvation, the only Name given under heaven whereby men may be saved.

This anti-Hindu and anti-Brahmin party has created a vacuum in religious faith and Christianity can fill that vacuum if evangelism is carried out strictly through indigenous methods. The city of Madras which the DMK first took over, and the state of Tamilnadu, today are fertile fields for the spread of Christianity. We of the Evangelical Church of India, have undoubtedly been taking advantage of it.

CHAPTER II—URBANIZATION IN MODERN INDIA ILLUSTRATED FROM MADRAS CITY

A. CHRISTIANITY AND CITIES

I do not have to impress my readers with the importance of cities in the history of the Church. Christianity was born, cradled, and brought up in the Mediterranean cities of the first century of the Christian era.

> The followers of Christ were first called Christians in a city; and the cities of the Graeco-Roman world became the channels of the saving Gospel of Jesus Christ. (Cornelius 1971:1)

Dr. Latourette (1953:75) one of the outstanding authorities of our time on the history of the Church says :

> At the outset, Christianity was predominantly urban; it moved along the trade routes from city to city. By the second century in at least some parts of Asia Minor it had spread widely into towns and even the countryside but its strength was in the cities which were so prominent a feature of the Roman Empire. (1953:75)

Cities were strategically important for evangelization and for the multiplying of churches throughout history of because they have been and are strategic centers of politics, trade, and industry. But never before in the history of mankind have the cities been so important as they are now in the twentieth century. Never before has there been a greater challenge than the Church is facing today in discipling the urban populations and multiplying churches among them. In the last chapter of this book is I shall be dealing with the principles and strategies that apply to urban church planting. In this chapter I shall confine my discussion to anthropological and sociological characteristics of an urbanized community in India. I write from a purely academic point of view with special reference to Madras City immigrants among whom the OMS has planted churches.

B. Urbanization and Urbanism

The two terms "urbanism" and "urbanization" are not merely evocative in the vocabulary of sociology, but are dynamic concepts denoting the life of the modern man who is in the grip of modernization. For thousands of years, the vast majority of people in the world were living a relatively isolated and static life. Farming was the main source of livelihood.

But the industrialization that suddenly appeared in the eighteenth and nineteenth century infused a dynamism into these tradition-bound people and provided no opportunity to return to their earlier quietude. Industrialization coupled with urbanism has been bringing different peoples together and shaping their way of life into a set pattern. Diversity of cultures was the life blood of the peasantry. But, culture is becoming uniform for modern industrial urban communities. (Ishwaran 1964:1)

This is what we call urbanism and urbanization. Some sociologists try to keep both the terms distinct while others use them interchangeably. Ernest Bengel contends that the term urbanization may be considered as a dynamic process and urbanism as a phenomenon or set of circumstances which have been brought out through the process of urbanization. (1955:10)

Without overstating the situation, we may say that the people the world over are in the grip of this new way of urban life. According to Harvey Cox (1966:273). "Future historians will record the twentieth century as the century in which the whole world became one immense city." Behind this exaggerated but still valid statement, lies the statistic that by the end of this century 50 per cent of the population of the world will be urban. "It is believed," says Wagner (1971:179) "that in India alone, the year 2,000 will see twenty cities of over twenty million each."

Let us see here briefly by what measure this rapid urbanization is taking place in India.

C. Independence and After

India has been witnessing a phenomenal shift of the rural population to towns since 1941. After World War II and since Independence, the rate of urbanization has been rapidly increasing as a result of industrial revolution in the country.

25

1. Democratic, Secular and Social Outlook

Though Mahatma Gandhi played a vital role in bringing freedom to India, yet he could not rationally guide the people of India in their search for a cultural and political foundation to the newly-born nation. Strangely enough, before and after Independence, the Mahatma kept harping on his *"Ram Rajya"* (Kingdom of Rama, as a synonym to the Kingdom of God) as his political philosophy; and was quite opposed to modern scientific methods, urbanization and industrialization of India emphasizing that salvation for India was in villages and not in cities.

Mahatma Gandhi, however, was suddenly removed from the Indian scene. This left Pandit Jawaharlal Nehru with a free hand to determine the future of the country. He emerged as the sole, undisputed leader who was to guide the destiny of the people of this great nation. Nehru was India and India was Nehru. (Woytinsky 1969:19)

Nehru, having been influenced by the West became wedded to Western rationalism, and the Western type of government. Though he was a true patriot and a devout servant of India he could not resist the inner attraction of the Western scientific approach to life. Twelve years before becoming a Prime Minister he wrote :

> I have become a queer mixture of the East and the West, out of place everywhere, at home, nowhere. Perhaps my thoughts and approach to life are more akin to what is called western than eastern, but India clings to me as she does to all of her children, in innumerable ways......
> I am a stranger and alien to the West. I cannot be of it. But in my country also I have an exile's feelings. (Nehru 1941:353)

In this dictum of Nehru we catch a glimpse of the direction in which the country was to go and of the shape of things to come after Independence.

The constitution was drafted and on January 26, 1950. India became a secular, democratic and republican state. Though India was predominantly a religious country the irony was that she was democratically ruled by a leader who called himself an agnostic. India is a secular country today because of Nehru.

The constitution, nonetheless has often been attacked by the communal parties, like the Jana Sangh, for its tenets of secularism. M. S. Golwalkar (1966:277) a staunch leader of RSS (*Rastriya Serak Samaj*) felt that :

> Our constitution, too, is just a cumbersome and heterogeneous, piecing together of various articles from various constitutions of western countries. It has absolutely nothing which can be called our own. Is there a single word of reference in its guiding principles as to what our national mission is and what our keynote in life is ?

Whether Mr. Golwalkar liked it or not, under Nehru's leadership the country was not to go back to the Vedic period, but march forward with the times.

2. The Industrial Revolution.

With this kind of constitutional background, a stage was set for a "New India." Pandit Jawaharlal Nehru and his government determined to drive away ignorance, poverty and unemployment through secular democratic and socialistic principles. He believed (or was made to believe by his advisors) that the objectives could be achieved only through industrialization of the country.

3. Heavy Industries and the Five-Year Plans

Nehru was also convinced that the key to economic progress lay in the heavy industries which would in turn set in motion the small-scale industries and revolutionize trade and agriculture. W. S. Woytinsky quotes (1969:174) what Nehru had said in the National Development Council of the second five-year plan in January, 1956 :

> If you want India to industrialize and to go ahead...you must industrialize and not putter about with old little factories producing hair

oil and the like. It is totally immaterial what
the things are whether they are small or big
consumer articles. You must go to the root
and base and build up the root on which you
will build up the structure of Industrial growth.
Therefore, it is the heavy industries that
count...We want planning for heavy-machine-
making industries.

Nehru boldly launched out on this gigantic task. But he was not
left without criticism. The first and second five-year plans did
not produce the results anticipated. While the heavy industries
had envisaged a 49 per cent increase in industrial output.
Achievement was only 39 per cent. At any rate, the industries
have set in motion a great revolution both in the public and in the
private sector. Nehru as a typical agnostic called the industries
and factories the "modern temples" of India making a shift
from the deeply superstitious thinking of the people to more of a
materialistic approach to life.

4. The Impact of Industrialization

Nehru's five-year plans were not solely responsible for the
industrialization of the country. But undoubtedly the policies of
the government to build up national economy through industries
with rigid restrictions on imports revolutionized the overall
patterns of life. People leaving behind the rural situations and
old ways of life began moving toward cities or else the cities
moved toward them. The major cities spread across their environs. New cities and towns began to rise. New jobs opened up
for the people. The job holders and their dependents began to
migrate to the "cities of refuge."

D. THE MIGRATION PATTERNS

Rural-to-urban migration in India is not negligible, but is a
very widespread phenomenon. Streams of migrations are flowing
not only toward the largest cities, but also to the hundreds of
medium-sized and smaller cities in all regions. Donald J. Bogue
and K. C. Zachariah who have conducted a special study in Indian
cities come out with the following conclusions :

    (a) Although originally this migration may have been
        "pioneering" movements, comprised predominantly

of males, the 1941—1951 decade witnessed the removal to cities of almost as many women as men. (This is very much like what was found in the interviews I had with the migrants to Madras).

(b) Unemployment data suggests the immigrants came seeking fortunes in cities.

(c) This upswing in urbanward migration probably is a fairly recent phenomenon which began in the late 1930's. It has now progressed to a point where the residents of almost every village have relatives or fellow villagers living in at least one, and possibly several, of the major cities. Family and village ties are sufficiently strong to create an obligation upon the successful migrant to help sponsor new entrants to the city. (Bogue 1962:45)

The above mentioned features are very common among immigrants in Madras City, who are members of our congregations.

E. Some Factors of Trends Among The Immigrants to Madras

Certain problems, causes for migration, and other factors, which have been observed among the dwellers in the city of Madras, are quite common among immigrants to any city in India, or for that matter among the immigrants to cities all over the world. But I shall project them as from the city of Madras.

1. "Push" and "Pull" Factors

Both push and pull factors have had an impact upon the movement of rural aud village populations into urban areas. The following table shows the percentage of rural, urban population of India every ten years from 1921 to 1971.

% of Population	1921	1931	1941	1951	1961	1971
Rural	18·8	88 0	86·0	82·0	82·0	80·1
Urban	11·2	12·0	13·9	17·3	18·0	19·9

In the city of Madras, the following statistics show the rate in which the city is growing :

1961—1,729,141

1971—2,469,449—42·81% growth

29

People in the rural areas often would say to themselves, "village says go go, city says come come." The village kicks the people out while cities welcome them all. There is a legend among the villagers that if they go to Madras or Coimbatore, they could earn a fortune.

Overpopulation in rural areas, which has implications in terms of available food or work, too little opportunity for securing enough land to produce a living, and reduced opportunities in business and employment are the "push" factors which forces rural residents to migrate to urban areas.

The city of Madras the largest city in Tamilnadu, Kerala, Andhra and Mysore has the strongest pull for the southerners, particularly Tamilians who come seeking employment.

A famine, depression, failure of crops in the rural areas pushes the villagers to the city. The industrial areas of the Madras City attracts people even during construction days, then later on as workers are needed for running plants and machinery.

2. Unemployment and Adverse Economic Conditions

A large percentage of immigrants move to the city seeking employment. Among the people of our city congregations interviewed, 15 per cent came to the city looking for jobs without even knowing where they were going to get their next meal.

3. Dependency

Dependency is a common factor in India. Usually only one member in the family is earning while the rest of the members of the family survive as natural dependents, hangers-on, and parasites. This is a phenomenon in the urban situation.

When one young man manages to get a job in the Madras city and firmly establishes himself he brings in his brothers cousins and others. He then goes back to the village and brings a wife. Now he has another group of people from her family, waiting to "somehow" get to Madras.

4. Looking for Educational Facilities

Lack of educational facilities in the villages drive the people to the cities. In most of our families there will always be some boy or girl from the village staying with their uncles and aunts, brothers and sisters attending some college or school of technology.

5. Transfers and "Floating Migrants"

Government employees or railway workers are transferred from city to city. For example, between 1965 and 1967, we had an efficient Christian brother Mr. Joseph Singh, as treasurer of our church at Kilpauk. Being a civilian in the army, when the order came for Mr. Joseph Singh, to move, he had to suddenly leave us. But, during the year he was with us he made a valuable contribution to the church. The city church, however, cannot rely upon this kind of "floating migrant" for its survival.

6. Permanent Residents

Though Madras is a cosmopolitan city with migrants from all over the country, most are from within the state and nearby districts. Certain people call themselves natives of Madras. Notable among these are the remarkable hard working Harijans who are the landless working people and have migrated to the city from the nearby districts of Chinglepet and Arcot. Most of them arrived here several generations ago. It would be proper to call them "early settlers." They are permanent residents.

These Harijan settlers are more numerous than other caste groups, around the suburban villages of Madras. As these people witnessed industrial and urban development in and around Madras and as they observed the new settlers earning their wealth quite rapidly, they were put under constant pressures for change and were looking for "lift," emancipation and liberation from centuries-old suppression. When the Gospel is preached to them, many have rapidly responded; while others who may not positively respond to the Gospel, do not oppossit it.

7. City-Village Ties

During the first few years, newcomers to the city often go back to their villages for festivals and marriages. As years go by

31

they tend to visit less often. Strong family ties are broken which results in a lack of family cohesion. However, when immigrants earn good money they usually go back to their villages to buy a field or a house to impress fellow villagers with their wealth.

> Such city dwellers dream of earning enough to
> go back to be 'big shots' in the little village.
> But this come-and-go business is a transitional
> phenomenon. Larger and larger numbers are
> becoming permanent residents of the city.
> (McGavaran 1970:279)

Nevertheless, there is still a strong tie between the city and the village. Though some might finally choose to settle in the city, yet number of migrants look forward to going back to their native places after retirement to "lay down their heads" in the villages of their birth. Such, periodically visit their villages for planting of crops and for harvests or else maybe on summer vacation. People movements have occurred back in the villages through these channels. I shall mention this more in detail in another chapter.

8. Continuity and Discontinuity of Culture

It is a common scene in all cities in India that the migrating families, and caste groups bring along with them their culture, customs, castes, and the village gods. Some they leave behind but most they bring with them. So much so that there is a fusion of different cultures, and they are under constant pressures for change.

Step by step many of the outer and superficial aspects of caste begin to break. On many occasions people who belong to different castes sit and dine together. Very few try to fulfill their caste duties and rituals. More and more people are giving up their caste labors and are turning their hands to any job which will fetch a better salary. On the whole, the outward rigidity of the caste system appears to be breaking up in urban areas. A city clerk told sociologist Kathleen Gough, "when I go to the office I put on my shirt and take off my caste, when I come home,

32

I take off my shirt and put on my caste." (Taya Zinkin 1962:51)
This sums up the position of caste today in the cities. The same
thing may also be told of Christians. With a very few exceptions,
the Christians of Madras still marry within their castes. The
dowry systems and several other customs, however, are not so
strictly observed. At a deeper level, however, caste is still strong.
Marriage is 99 per cent within the caste and sub-caste. Men vote
for candidates of their caste. They get jobs for their caste fellows
not for others. Brahmins hold themselves entirely separate.
Vellalas do not want to be confused with *Harijans*. *Chettis* do
not like to be considered *Vellalas*. Even Christians take pride in
remembering that they are Nadar, Syrian, or Melas. Most
Christian marriages are with people of the correct "background."
These deep-seated cleavages have a great bearing on the spread of
the Gospel.

Theoretically people within the context of continuity and
discontinuity of culture and having been cut off from traditions
ought to respond to the Gospel better than villagers. This has
proved true to a certain extent in our church planting ministry in
Madras. However, the hard fact is that (except in Pentecostal
denominations to a small extent) "conversions from a casteless
city society" proves to be a myth. It is not occurring. It will
not occur to any appreciable extent. Most people who become
Christian join their caste fellows inside one-caste churches. They
do not join conglomerate congregations nearly so readily.

9. Socio-Economic Problems

As villagers migrate to the city of Madras they come
expecting a life of ease and pleasure. Whereas in their villages
they ate what they grew and bought very little. In the city they
have to buy almost everything, including water. The rented
homes, the high cost of living, the rates, this bill and that bill
strain their budgets. Added to this burden are the unemployed
relatives and other hangers-on. Uninvited guests from the villages
make the head of the family borrow money from the *Marvadi*
(money lending caste) month after month. Utensils and silver
ornaments are mortgaged.

Among employees, there are always tensions, strikes and
lock-outs, and corruption in high places. There is a decline of

moral and social standards. While back in small villages, the life of the individual is constantly watched by every one, in a large city he is one among the thousands. There are all sorts of evil attractions by which a man can spoil his life. There is no limit to which young people can ruin their lives.

On the other hand, many who belong to the so-called low caste group with poor monthly income, live a simple life. Inspite of that they also seek after pleasure and sinful life in their own way.

But in the midst of all this sinful urban world, some hungry souls have found the Saviour. There have been conversions from all the classes of people. It is from the Harijan community, however, that most converts came as families into the Church. Of our thirty five churches, eighteen are solidly from the Harijans.

10. The Christian Migrants.

Among all the others who rush to the city, the Christians of Tamilnadu are those who are in the front line. Our C^3 Christians are all those who are from such nominal Christians who happened to settle near any one of our churches in the city. The Christian migrants include those of Harijans and Vellalas background from Chinglepet, North Arcot and Tanjore Districts and Nadar background from Tirunelveli District.

The Nadars of Tirunelveli began to migrate early in this century. In 1938, a survey was conducted among Christians in Tirunelveli. It showed 8 per cent of the members had migrated as traders, laborers, domestic servants, public servants, clerk and mechanics. The reasons for the immigrations were :

    a. economic pressure

    b. the immigration habit

    c. the enterprising spirit of the Nadar Christians (Sargant 1962,128)

There is always a brain drain in the city. Our churches do have quite a few talented C^2 Christians. Some very able men handle the administration of the church. They are mostly C^2 Vellala Christians from Tanjore District.

I now turn to a brief background study of the other churches and denominations in Madras.

CHAPTER III—CHRISTIAN MISSIONS IN MADRAS
A. CHRISTIANITY AND OTHER RELIGIONS IN MADRAS

Name of Religion	1961 Population	%	1971 Population	%	% of Inc./Decr.
Boddhism ...	336	·02	678	·03	+ 85·25
Christianity ...	119,282	6·90	163,573	6·62	+ 37·13
Hinduism ...	1,469,061	84·96	2,076,500	84 09	+ 41·35
Islam ...	129,463	7·49	210,083	8·51	+ 62·27
Jainism ...	9,041	·52	17,164	·69	+ 89·85
Sikhism ...	710	·04	1,311	·05	+ 84·65
Other Religions ...	1,214	·07	140	·01	— 88·47
Total ...	1,729,137	100·00	2,469,449	100 00	+ 42·81

I shall now trace the history of the 6·6 per cent Christians in Madras. One can write several hundred pages about the History of Christian Missions in India. But that may not be in line with the purpose and the main thrust of this book. At the same time if I just make a passing reference it might appear as though I am trying to under estimate or ignore the presence of these other denominations. Hence this chapter.

B. ST. THOMAS TRADITIONS

Pundit Jawaharlal Nehru, referring to the St. Thomas tradition once said:

> Christianity is as old in India as Christianity itself. Christianity found its roots in India before it went to countries like England, Portugal and Spain. Christianity is as much a religion of the Indian soil as any other religion of India. (Levai 1971 : 84)

35

While Peter was a Bishop in Rome, Paul was preaching in Corinth and St. Thomas was preaching the Gospel in South India. This tradition may be supported to a degree by evidence from the early historical records, the writings of Marco Polo, and from the Acts of St. Thomas etc. (Moraes 1964:25-26)

According to the tradition, after establishing "seven and a half" churches in Malabar Coast, St. Thomas came to Madras and died as a martyr at the hands of the Brahmins. Some Christian scholars think the great Tamil poet, Thiruvalluvar, who lived somewhere during the first century, was influenced by St. Thomas.

Atleast three historical places in the city of Madras stand in the memory of St. Thomas. The first one is the landmark of the city, St. Thomas Mount from where the famous Mount Road leads northeast into the main city. During the fifteenth century, the Portuguese excavated at this mount a "bleeding cross" with an old Sassanian Pehdevi inscription on it (it also had spots that looked like blood stains and which reappeared after being scrubbed away). A little chapel has been built on top of this hill. (Smith 1893:26)

The second is "the little mount" between Guindy and Saidapet where St. Thomas is said to have performed miracles and caused water to come out of a rock by striking it, to quench the thirst of the people who gathered to hear him preach. The opening in the rock is still there with water gushing out of it! It is believed that the water has curative power.

The third is the San Thome Cathedral by the beach, where St. Thomas is supposed to have been buried.

Though there appears to have been no visible churches that he might have founded in Madras, this Thomas Tradition at least leads many to believe that Christianity came to India in the first century long before sixteenth the Portuguese who arrived in the century.

C. Roman Catholic Churches

History will long remember the Jesuit missionaries for their contribution to the Christian Church.

Francis Xavier who landed in Goa in May, 1542, at the age of 36, spread his ministry to all the coastal areas of both the Eastern and Western cost. He won many fisher folks in the Nagapatinam and Coramandel Coast. Even today many fishing villages are solidly Roman Catholic. The definitely lack and have long lacked good teaching from God's Word, but it is very interesting to observe that nevertheless these converts have endured all kinds of difficulties and today form a major part of the Roman Catholic community in India.

Through the centuries, conversions also took place among people of all castes. With these converts and their descendants and with Catholic immigrants to Madras City, today Roman Catholic membership is 109,185. This figure does not include thousands who have no church affiliation but would still call themselves Catholics. The chart on the following page gives statistics on the Catholic Churches in Madras. It is interesting to observe the forty-seven "fields" opened by the Roman Catholic City Churches. Apparently, the Catholics are finding Madras and its environs fruitful for church planting.

D. THE ARMENIAN TRADITION

Available records do not state the exact year when Armenians first arrived in the Coromandel Coast, but evidences exist of their trading in South India in the early part of the sixteenth century. The early Armenian settlers were soon followed by others from Iran end in the seventeenth and eighteenth centuries, a flourishing colony of Armenian merchants was well established in Madras.

An Armenian church was first built somewhere in the seventeenth century in the Esplanade area, but appears to have been destroyed as the authorities did not permit continued use of it in the fort area.

The present Armenian Church of the Virgin Mary, situated in No. 2, Armenian Street, George Town, Madras, was constructed in 1912. The land on which this edifice stands was being used as a burial ground for the community and in the early days before the present church was erected, a small chapel in its

Name of the Parishes.	Members.	Priests & Work.	Asso.	Schools & Teach.	Fields Open- by Parishes.
1. Santhome	*	2	4	7	1
2. Adyar	1,200	2	...	2	6
3. Asoknager	2,000	1	3	...	...
4. Rayapettah	4,100	4	3	7	1
5. Raja Annamalipuram.	3,000	2	8	6	...
6. Mylapore	2,592	2	3	5	...
7. Nungambakkam	4,378	2	2	6	1
8. Kodambakkam	3,200	3	11	6	...
9. Kilpauk	*	3	5	6	...
10. Armenian Street	350	10	2	3	...
11. Chintadripet	3,000	3	2	3	...
12. Broadway	3,750	5	6	7	4
13. George Town	2,425	2	3	2	...
14. Narasingapuram	1,104	1	2	...	...
15. Park Town	400	1	3	...	...
16. Royapuram	2,100	2	1	2	...
17. Royapuram	3,000	3	4	3	...
18. Washermanpet	2,800	1	4	...	...
19. Ayanavaram	4,100	2	1	...	1
20. Basin Bridge	1,910	2	4	1	...
21. Egmore	2,250	1	5	2	4
22. Perambur	10,000	11	1	8	2
23. Vepery	4,000	3	11	6	2
24. Vepery	*	3	3	4	...
25. Vyasarpady	5,600	8	3	3	8
26. Pudupet	3,781	2	3	5	...
27. Ennore	1,550	3	1	4	3
28. Kasimode	5,650	6	...	3	...
29. Madhavaram	2,000	3	...	2	3
30. Tiruvottiyur	2,500	2	2	3	...
31. Tandiarpet	1,750	2	2	...	...
32. Chrompet	2,200	1	4	3	...
33. Darkast (Ahakputhur).	625	1	...	2	...
34. Meenambakkam	900	2	2	1	...
35. Pallavaram	3,500	4	3	6	3
36. Poonamallee	2,020	2	2	...	6
37. St. Thomas Mount	8,500	4	4	9	...
38. Saidapet	3,520	2	3	...	1
39. Thambaram	3,430	2	2	5	1
Total	109,185	115	122	133	47

* Not received.

Fig. 2.—Roman Catholic Churches In Madras.

precincts was being used as a place for community worship. The belfry tower contains six beautiful bells which are reputed to be the biggest in Madras, were cast in England during the eighteenth and nineteenth centuries.

Worship in this church ceased long ago because Armenians ceased living in Madras The property was for many years under the possession of a private company and after an order of the High Court of Madras is now under the trusteeship of the Armenian Association of India. All this is a clear case of a "dead church"—it did not seek to plant any daughter churches among the Tamilians and it died. The Armenian merchant princes in Madras were rich and influential during the seventeenth century. They were reputed to have built roads and bridges for Madras, but they never used their influence to multiply Armenian Churches among other ethnic units in the city.

E. CSI CHURCHES - BEFORE UNION

The main line Protestant Churches in Madras are united and have become the Church of South India with a total membership of 42,825, as against our ECI membership of 4,826. The union took place in 1947. I shall briefly discuses here the Christian missions and denominations in Madras before the union and shall then describe their position now.

1. Anglicans

In the course of the nineteenth century, wealthier English merchants acquired some land now known as Fort St. George. These men of the East India Company in order to have a place of worship built St. George's Cathedral which one might say became the mother church for the Anglicans in Madras. It was consecrated in 1816.

Though originally churches were established for the European settlers, their Ang'o-Indian descendants and English missionaries who came worked among the Tamilians. After a Tamil congregation was formed, Tucker Church was built in 1818–1820. Later a few other churches also were erected.

2. Presbyterians

Soon after 1813, members of the Church of Scotland working in India as merchants or soldiers decided to have *kirks* built in the different Presidencies. The first was built in Calcutta. Soon after that, the present, beautiful Scotch Kirk was built in Madras. In 1906, a Brahmin and his wife and four children were recorded as being baptized in it. The Church did much social work in the city, but not much church planting evangelism. There were a few conversions.

3. Congregationalists

The London Missionary Society began its work in Madras in 1805. In 1819, the " Missionary Chapel " in Mukkathal Street was built. LMS missionaries were very energetic in evangelism and also established a few churches inside and outside Madras.

4. British Methodists

Wesleyan Methodism was brought to India in 1814 by Thomas Coke. He gave all his personal fortune to mission work and died at sea on his way to Ceylon and India. The Methodist Missionary Society was formed in 1819 in London. Rayapettah Wesley Church was established in 1818 ; Tamil Wesley Broadway was established in 1861. In 1903, there was a circuit of five Wesleyan Methodist Churches.

F. THE MADRAS CSI CHURCHES SINCE UNION (1947)

The Roman Catholic Missions in India, which came under various Societies and Orders, yet belonged to one and the same Church. But in the case of Protestant " Missions " (by which I mean also denominations) because of their ecclesiastical and doctrinal differences back in their own countries, there was no common ground on which the union could be brought about

However, in the wake of national movement, some thoughtful leaders felt the need to bring all the denominations under one umbrella. This came about in several stages. The seed for the union was sown early this century. In 1901, the first definite achievement of the union of Presbyterians in South India took place. This brought together the American Arcot Mission and its denomination, the Church of Scotland, and the Free Church of Scotland in and around Madras. (Fifth 1961 : 232) The union movement, step-by-step, gained support and in 1947 a visible, organic union of the Congregational, Reformed, Methodist and Anglican denominations took place. The CSI came into existence.

This union has brought a solidarity among Christians in South India, and made the churches and denominations recognize their common goal and vision. Union has also fortified the political position of Christians in a predominantly non-Christian country. One other benefit of this union was that church properties were safeguarded.

The most disappointing outcome, however, is that CSI Churches in Madras are not evangelizing. They appear to show little concern for the salvation of the people around them. *The charts on the next two pages** show that only six out of forty-six churches have been established since 1947. When it is remembered that these six new congregations have been created only to church the CSI immigrants to the city (and not to liberate non-Christians into the liberty of Christ), the almost total disinterest of CSI in evangelism may be realized. As I have already said, the Roman Catholics have opened forty-seven fields around Madras. This kind of negligence to multiply churches among non-Christians is a common phenomenon among the Protestant churches in India. We should be ashamed of ourselves about this state of affairs. If the main line Protestant Churches are not going to actively get involved in discipling India's responsive population, there will be no significant spread of the Good News in the land of India.

G. THE NON-CSI CHURCHES

1. Lutherans

Ziegenbalag and Plutschau landed in Tranquebar in 1706. Though they were ridiculed by British merchants at first, the

---

* Complied by Rev: P. J. Sadhusingh by a visit to each church,

Church of South India (CSI)

Name of CSI Congregation	Date of Established	Total Christian Communities	Confirmation Candidates	Baptisms 1-10-1870—39-9-1972	Children Sunday School	Christian Young Men
1. Anderson Church	1859	248	1	9	23	5
2. Tamil Wesley, Broadway.	1861	629	10	47	63	40
3. Christ Church, Washermanpet & Korukupet.	1846	1,158	2	80	217	62
4. David Son Church	1805	149	4	8	35	11
5. English Circuit of Wesley Churches.	1903	447	—	—	128	27
6. Harwood Raw Memorial.	—	1,120	7	78	126	30
7. Holicross & St. Michael's	—	(Information not
8. Labonon Puram	—	608	—	13	98	25
9. Missionary Chapel	1819	1,070	4	38	162	32
10. Nellore, Bitragunta	1939	175	—	6	38	7
11. Perampeer Wesley	1905	2,185	32	112	318	32
12. Red Hills & Ponneri	—	1,082	70	179	322	77
13. Royapuram	1879	844	1	60	162	25
14. St. Andrew's, Choolai.	1873	769	7	29	66	17
15. St. Matthias	1825	675	—	50	50	15
16. St. Mark's. G.T.	1805	452	—	18	123	11
17. St. Paul's, Vepery	1858	2.140	1	128	191	17
18. Trinity	1831	169	—	6	—	—
19. Tucker Church	1820	577	—	10	144	45
20. Tangal & Tondiarpet.	1922	620	3	67	227	—
21. V.V.K. Unit	1959	546	6	27	69	18

* lay preacher or teacher - catechist

in Madras City 1972

Christian Young Women	Non-Christ. Youth	Women Fellowship	Men's Group	Newcomers To Congre.	Past. Inc. Thru Giving 1-4-71 —31-3-72	Workers and Pastors	Hospitals, Colleges and Schools
10	—	25	—	21	5,000	1	
—	2	28	—	57	8,000	1	Anderson Girls' High School
55	—	68	—	25	4,970	1	Northwick
—	1	10	12	25	4,700	1	St. Paul's High School
28	—	27	—	9	80,648	1	Bain's School
12	—	25	—	18	13,500	1	Corley High School
obtained)							Kellect High School
—	—	32	—	3	—	—	Monahan High School
15	—	30	—	27	21,573	*	Bendwick High School
8	2	—	—	7	3,800	1	St. Ebbas High School
—	—	42	—	45	14,684	1	St. Thomas High School
45	5	125	20	28	5,085	1	Ewart High School
10	—	124	—	57	24,444	*	Schools for deaf in Santhom
—	—	28	—	85	32,350	1	St. Christopher Teacher's Training College
116	15	—	—	25	15,500	1	Christian College
9	—	20	—	15	8,606	1	Kalyani Hospital
15	—	70	40	60	31,000	1	Reni Hospital
—	—	—	—	6	2,236	1	etc., etc., etc.
15	—	60	—	—	6,622	1	
—	—	—	12	10	26,035	1	
—	—	7	—	8	5,440	*	

** Pastorate income given in rupees

Name of CSI Congregation	Date of Established	Total Christian Communities	Confirmation Candidates	Baptisms 1–10–1870—30–9–1972	Children Sunday School	Christian Young Men
22. Ayanavaram	1968	1,735	16	54	130	20
23. Avadi	—	1,487	12	89	223	45
24. Ambattur	—	947	26	89	148	74
25. Aminjikarai & Nerkundram.	—	1,153	17	72	225	35
26. Adayar	1967	441	5	10	105	28
27. Christ Church— Alandur.	1883	1,084	4	39	167	15
28. Christ Church— Mount Road.	1852	496	—	30	134	12
29. Good Shepherd Church.	—	1,442	3	54	124	40
30. Kodambakkam Church.	1963	1,821	13	64	270	77
31. Malayalam Church	1947	1,005	—	21	145	60
32. Poonamalli (South)	—	1,712	12	106	387	119
33. Rayapettai (Wesley)	1818	1,377	2	72	203	20
34. St. Andrew, Kirk— Egmore,	1821	267	2	9	32	15
35. St. Mary's Church (Fort).	1680	110	—	6	136	—
36. St. Thomas (Santhome) English.	—	254	—	18	241	10
37. St. Thomas (Santhome) Tamil.	1858	790	12	27	73	24
38. St. Thomas Mt. Tamil Wesley.	—	1,331	25	72	169	36
39. St. Thomas Mt. St. Stephen,	1823	463	—	12	118	50
40. St. George's Cathedral.	1816	1,440	—	31	45	25
41. St. John's—Egmore	1842	1,240	—	37	583	20
42. Triplicane, Mylapore (Pastorate).	—	460	—	29	54	68
43. Tambaram (CSI)	1940	2,484	23	128	81	40
44. Zion Church	1847	1,086	—	67	480	35
45. Pallavaram Unit	—	1,185	28	—	31	115
46. Saidapet Unit	1920	1,352	—	68	84	6
Total ...		42,825	348	2,169	6,950	1,485

Note :—56% of church income sent to the central fund.

Christian Young Women	Non-Christ. Women Youth	Women Fellowship	Men's Group	Newcomers To Congre.	Past. Inc. Thru Giving 1-4-71 —31-3-72	Workers and Pastors	Hospitals, Colleges and Schools
30	1	35	—	53	31,150	1	
25	1	55	—	45	11,374	1	
35	5	83	—	34	1,300	1	
20	8	40	—	10	14,000	1	
10	1	22	—	19	13,694	1	
10	—	15	—	33	23,642	1	
10	—	30	—	16	25,708	1	
32	3	165	—	30	37,054	1	
39	2	94	37	49	36,995	1	
35	2	95	—	15	29,430	1	
7	15	96	94	30	8,236	1	
12	—	72	—	40	28,470	1	
5	20	—	—	20	31,188	1	
—	—	—	—	50	22,000	1	
5	25	—	—	10	83,000	1	
—	—	34	—	43	13,500	1	
26	—	35	—	20	9,423	1	
95	—	75	—	38	50,000	1	
30	—	30	—	30	29,679	1	
10	—	20	—	20	15,899	1	
21	2	142	21	62	24,000	1	
70	—	50	—	40	34,000	1	
5	—	68	—	70	17,995	1	
40	—	90	50	111	2,200	1	
12	—	18	6	8	26,000	1	
922	110	2,075	292	1,427	939,132	46	

English chaplains in Madras encouraged their work. Ziegenbalag once spent half a year in Madras City preaching to natives in Tamil.

The Lutheran Adaikalanathar Church in Purasawalkam was founded in 1848, By 1971, it had congregation of 2,500 members, 1,700 communicants. It has drawn people from all castes. In 1952, this church branched out to the Kilpauk area. The new church is known as Arulnathar Church.

There are also other churches of the Lutheran Federation, like Arcort Lutheran, Missouri Synod Lutheran. etc.

2. The Syrian Churches

There is one old Orthodox Syrian Church in the Old Town Broadway. The Reformed Mar Thomas Syrian Church also has a sanctuary in Chetpet. St. Thomas Evangelical Church has its little congregation which meets in a rented hall.

3. Emmanuel Methodist Church

This is a very large Methodist English-speaking congregation. Ever since Rev. Schneck and Rev. Dr. Samuel Kamalesan, became pastors of this congregation, the Church experienced a tremendous growth. In 1950, the communicants were about twenty-five, but by 1972, had increased to 400 and the total Christian community is now around 1,200.

A sister church of Emmanuel, the Tamil Methodist Church has about 500 communicants and a community of 942. With its present pastor, Rev. Mohan, a Yeotmal graduate, the church is making good progress.

4. The Salvation Army

In the early days of ministry, it was concentrating on the high caste Hindus without any success. Then Commissioner Booth Tucker realized that the Lord had called the Salvationists to work among the Depressed Classes. Their success, however, was mostly in Andhra Pradesh. In Madras, they did not find a way to multiply churches amongst the Depressed Class. At

46

present there is only one Salvation Army cangregation and it consists of second and third generation immigrants from Andhra and the worship is in English.

5. Plymouth Brethren

Mr Handley Bird from England organized a Brethren Assembly in the early twenties in the Old City in a rented place at 17, Broadway. Later it was moved to Vepery. Smaller assemblies were started by lay people in Royapuram, Chetpet, Triplicane, Ambathur, St. Thomas Mount and Maduravoil.

6. American Advent Mission

It began early this century. These evangelical churches, thirty in number are all very near self-support.

7. Telugu Baptist Churches

In 1878, Lyman Jewett first started the work in Madras. Rev. G. Cornelius, who has done an extensive research among the Telugu Baptist Churches gives the following information :

Centers Belonging to and Churches Associated With Madras Telugu Baptist, Church (Commonly Called Vepery Church).

	Section Name	Name of the Center or Church	Number of Families
1.	Kondithope (Royapuram)	Royapuram Center	55
2.	Vepery (near the church premises)	Mother Church	50
3.	Chulai	Chulai Telugu Baptist Church	230
4.	Aseervadapuram	Aseervadapuram Center	131
5.	Krishnampet (Triplicane)	Triplicane Telugu Baptist Church	120
6.	Govindapuram	Govindapuram Center	5
7.	Basin Bridge (Mulakathalam)	Basin Bridge Center	35
8.	New Model Lines	Model Lines Center	64

Section Name	Name of the Center or Church	Number of Families
9. Anjeneya Nagar	Anjeneya Nagar Center	72
10. Periamet	Periamet Center	30
11. Puduppet	Puduppet Center	24
12. Gantz Road (Patalam)	Immanuel Telugu Baptist Church	100
13. K. K. Lines	K. K. Lines Center	10
14. Coronation Nagar	Coronation Nagar Center	35
15. Korukupet	Korukupet Center	29
16. Pulla Reddy Puram	Pulla Reddy Puram Center	57
17. Sothu Perambedu (Rural)	Sothu Perambedu Baptist Church	20
18. Gummadipundi (Rural)	Gummadipundi Baptist Church	10

Centers Belonging to and Churches Associated with the Perambur Telugu Baptist Church (Commonly Called Perambur Church).

Section Name	Name of the Center or Church	Number of Families
1. Cooks Road (church area)	Cooks Road Center	55
2. Mangalapuram	Mangalapuram Center	15
3. Akangipuram	Akangipuram Center	7
4. Pudunager (near Water Tank)	Ayanavaram Telugu Baptist Church	55
5. B & C Mill Lines	B & C Mill Lines	20
6. Arundatiyapalem	Arundatiyapalem	7
7. Sembium	Sembium Center	15

Section Name	Name of the Center or Church	Number of Families
8. Railway Quarters (Ayana-varam)	Railway Quarters Center	20
9. Aminjekarai	Aminjekarai Center	19
10. Villivakkam	Villivakkam Telugu Baptist Church	45
11. Nazarethpuram (Suburban) St. Thomas Mount	St. Thomas Mount Telugu Baptist Church	60
12. Nazarethpuram (Mala Section) St. Thomas Mount	Bethel Telugu Baptist Church	40
13. Mutta Puduppet (Sub-urban)	Telugu Baptist Church Mutta Puduppet	80
14. Pattabhiram (Suburban)	Telugu Baptist Church Pattabhiram	55
15. Kanyakapuram (Suburban) Avadi	The Israelpet Telugu Baptist Church	120

8. Madras English Baptist Church

A Baptist Society was formed in Madras in 1847. Soon after that the Baptist Church for the English-speaking was established. Missionaries of the American Baptist Society preached at this church for about 50 years. In 1937, for the first time a national, Rev. G. A. Baynes, became the minister of the Church. His son, Rev. J. A. L. Baynes is the present pastor.

9. Tamil Baptist Churches

There are four Tamil Baptist Churches in Madras. The state of these is not encouraging. However the Baptist Church at Kilpauk has about 200 membership. The pastor of the church, Rev. P. Devanesan, is known for his sanctified life.

10. The Pentecostal Denominations

The Pentecostal Churches are very vigorous. Notable among this group are : The Apostolic Christian Assembly, Zion Gospel Prayer House, Madras Pentecostal Assembly, and the Indian Pentecostal Church. Each of these denominations have several congregations, large and small. The Assembly of God, The Church of God in India, and the Ceylon Pentecostals also have a few churches in Madras.

11. Other Independent Churches

Among the several other idependent denominations, the church called "Jehovah Shammah" and the Laymen's Evangelical Fellowship deserve mention.

During 1938 and 1940, Bakta Singh, a Sikh convert from Punjab was ministering in Madras. People still say that during those days, the whole city was shaken. His ministry, However, was very effective among the nominal Christian community with few conversions from the non-Christians. Until 1940, Bhakta Singh had no intention of starting a church. But during the later months, he could not avoid opening some kind of an assembly as his converts were being persuaded by the Seventh Day Adventists, Jehovah's Witnesses and others to join their churches. The traditional denominations simply did not have the warmth of Christian fellowship and fervent belief these born-again children of God had experienced and wanted.

This little congregation first met in a rented home. Later it moved to a more spacious place, which subsequently the followers of Brother Bakta Singh bought. The new congregation is known as "Jehovah Shammah" (The Lord Has Heard). The membership is over 1,000. Baktha Singh has established a such assemblies all over India.

Just a little after the "Jehovah Shammah" movement in Madrs, a great man of God, Brother N. Daniel, a high school teacher from Andra Pradesh came to Madras in response to God's specific call. He first worked mostly among college students. He had been used of the Lord mightily all over South India.

Hundreds of nominal Christians surrendered their lives. As a little boy, I saw Christians raising their hands and crying out aloud to confess their sins in Brother Daniel's revival meetings.

In Madras he first started a little group known as Laymen's Evangelical Fellowship. It was originally a spiritual fellowship group for laymen but as years went by it turned into a denomination. Its ministry has spread into little towns all over Tamilnadu and Andhra State. The men who belong to this fellowship are known for their sanctified lives. They have also been accused-rightly of taking young Christians away from their families. But nobody can question their integrity and love for the Gospel.

H. MADRAS—HAS HAD SEVERAL REVIVALS

From the movements outside the main line churches I have been describing, it becomes clear that God also works outside the older denominations. When an individual surrenders his life completely to Him, and forms himself and his fellows into a church, God uses that person, whoever he may be, for His glory. "Whenever two or three are gathered together in my name, there am I in the midst."

The 1905 Revival in Tamilnadu about which Dr. Edwin Orr speaks in his book *Evangelical Awakening in India* was a part of a world-wide phenomenon. (1970 : 88–91) People were also praying for revival the same year in Madras. Madras has seen many revivals since then. In this city of awakenings, the Lord has raised the Evangelical Church of India through the ministry of OMS International. Mr. Raj Nelson, who has done an extensive study on the Madras churches has made an interesting observation about these churches. I shall quote it here before I go on to evaluate the history of this movement from the next chapter onward.

> In these Evangelical Church of India congregations, God is at work in a remarkable way. Pastors who have filled out my questionaires have stated that demons are cast out, sick people are healed through prayer, and slaves to alcohol have been delivered by the power of the

Gospel. This small, fast-growing denomination in Madras City has to be commended for its alignment with sound biblical principles of church growth. (Nelson 1973)

I. THE TRAGIC INDIFFERENCE TO MADRAS' RECEPTIVITY

With this glorious history of the past to the response of the Christian Gospel as it has been brought to the people of Madras and Tamilnadu, the Tamilians continue to be responsive. The Roman Catholics are taking advantage of it. The Pentecostals have found Madras to be fertile soil for their activities. We who belong to the Evangelical Church of India have attested to this receptivity. It is high time that the CSI and other Protestant Churches wake up to the remarkable spiritual hunger in Madras and its suburbs.

52

CHAPTER IV—THE OMS ENTERS MADRAS

Into such a deep-rooted, cultural, linguistic and political background, and into the situation and presence of both these conglomerate and free churches, the Oriental Missionary society officially entered Madras in the year 1953. I shall be dealing from this chapter onward with the Society's spectacular achievement of twenty years of church planting ministry. However, it becomes inevitable at this point to mention briefly the history of the OMS from its beginning to the present, tracing the stages by which the vision of the founder has reached India and finally to Madras and the other remote parts of India.

A. Brief Description of the OMS

1. The Founder

Charles E. Cowman, founder and first President of the Oriental Missionary Society was born in 1868, and died in 1924. He was led to the Lord through his own wife who had been converted just a month prior to her husband's new experience in Christ. Charles Cowman was a successful businessman in the Chicaco Telegraph Office. He was a traffic chief and later on became the wire chief of the New York Division of the Western Union Telegraphic Company. Charles Cowman began witnessing about Christ almost right after his conversion he had led seventy-five of his fellow workers to Christ. The movement continued to spread among the telegraph workers all over the United States. He soon organized his converts into the Telegrapher's Mission Band, which became she beginning group that paved the way toward the founding of the Oriental Missionary Society.

The Telegrapher's Mission Band met once a month in a hotel room and gave a monthly offering for missions. They all became men with great passion for souls. It was not long before the Lord gave Charles Cowman a vision for all types of evangelistic work. He participated in open-air services and Sunday School services. He took keen interest in slum missions. The following year after his conversion, he and his wife went as delegates from their Methodist Church to a national Epworth League Convention. This meeting made a great missionary awakening and he took a pledge for support of national workers. Then on September 3, 1894, he made an entry in his diary :

> Attended Dr. :Simpson's missionary convention and was searched through and through and bared and exposed and searched by God's searching Spirit. I took another step toward God. (1928 : 84)

During that meeting a piece of missionary literature on India was placed in his hand :

> . . . and he began reading of India's missions. It made a deep impression upon him and on his heart was rolled a burden that would not leave him, even after much prayer. He believed that the Lord was calling him to India, but he did not know what step to take to reach this dark land. (Ibid., 84)

Further, his wife did not feel called to India and the family physician said she could not live in such a trying climate.

The Cowman did consult with other of God's children and waited on God for a definite guidance. The Lord spoke to them His Word, "Stay thou :there, till I bring thee word." "Matt. 2:13) He did bring a word and the call came on August 11, 1900, at 10:30 A.M. to go as missionaries to Japan, not in a crowded gathering where there was a great wave of missionary enthusiasm, but in a hush of the Sunday morning worship. On the morning of February 1, 1901, Charless E. Cowman, the great missionary warrior, left the shores of the United States of America with his able wife and arrived in Japan the same month. The first entry in his notebook upon arrival was :

> Tokyo, Japan, February 22nd. A new era in our lives. New responsibilities, new hope, new avenues of thought, new subjects for prayer.

> Oh, for faith, unyielding faith! My soul yearns
> for a close alliance with God. (Ibid., 124)

Then on the following day, on February 23, the following promises were recorded in his diary :

> February 23rd. Promises claimed this morning:
> 'I will sanctify my great Name which was
> profaned among the heathen . . . and the heathen
> shall know that I am the Lord, when I shall
> be sanctified in you before their eyes.' 'I will
> give thee the treasures of darkness and the
> hidden riches of secret places, that thou mayest
> know that I, the Lord, which call thee by name,
> am the God of Israel.' What are we here for
> but to make known that God is the Lord?
> Gracious promises. What have we to fear, for
> God is with us and God have sent us! (Ibid.,
> 124)

Here was a man who launched out in a step of faith in response to God's call, like the Abraham of old and like William Carey the father of modern missions, Hudson Taylor and several others. There he went depending entirely upon God without the backing of any home church or mission and without knowing where he would get his next supply of goods. The step he had taken was indeed a great step of faith. And there followed in his footsteps hundreds and thousands of missionaries and national preachers and laymen. Today, OMS has extended its faith ministry to more than 11 countries all over the world with 299 missionary personnel both at home and abroad, 1,490 national workers, 549 students in the seminaries, 912 organized churches and 422 preaching points, with 205,690 full members and an annual expenditure of $2,673,044·01 (year ending March 31, 1970).

2. A Brief Survey of OMS History

Japan was the first country entered by the OMS. During the two world wars, the churches were completely wiped out. They were started all over again and today there are about one hundred, self-supporting, self-governing churches.

At the beginning of the century, a number of Koreans had migrated to Japan and were living there. From among this group, several came in contact with the Tokyo Bible Seminary of the OMS. They were trained in the Tokyo Seminary. Rev. E. A. Kilbourne, one of the early converts of Charles Cowman, who followed him to the field, made a survey of Korea. A group of Korean national evangelists, who were trained in the Tokyo Seminary were sent to Korea in 1907. Subsequently, a seminary was opened in Seoul. The head-quarters which was in Tokyo was shifted to Seoul and an all-out effort was made to evangelize South Korea. Churches were being established quite rapidly in those days when Korea was under the grip of a great revival movement. Dr. Edwin Orr is right, in saying that revival always drives men to proclaim the Gospel and to the planting of churches. The 1905 revival which swept the world made a tremendous impact on the Christians in Korea with the result that tne Korean nationals and the missionaries took up the challenge to establish churches. Dr. Duewel, the present President of the OMS, commenting about those early days of ministry in Korea says :

> Those were days of tremendous revival move-
> ments in Korea and the Society flourished
> rapidly . . . The Korean church has been known
> for its early morning prayer meetings which go
> back to the time of these great Korean revivals.
> The Korean church has been known as a
> zealous evangelizing church, laymen and pastors
> have carried tremendous prayer burdens for the
> congregations and for the unsaved. Their
> personal work and witnessing have won many
> to Christ. (1970:19)

The evangelistic thrust of the Mission has borne fruit so abundantly in Korea, more than in its operation in any other part of the world. Today there are more than 600 organized, self-supporting churches, and a government recognized Bible College with over 250 students with a Korean President, Dr. John Cho. The Korea Holiness Church has a great plan to bring the number of churches to one thousand by the end of this decade.

God enabled Charles E. Cowman in 1907, to begin work in China. Liu Ny Guam was the first Chinese who was trained in the OMS Tokyo Bible Seminary. He was then sent to Seoul. Ten other Chinese students were also sent with him to Seoul Seminary. This group of Chinese Christians and some missionaries arrived in China in 1921. There was a big seminary established in Shanghai in memory of Charles E. Cowman after he passed away in 1924. Several national churches were planted. However, there was a great setback in Christian witness in 1937, when the Japanese army invaded China. After the Communist takeover of China in 1948, the missionaries were all sent out, the properties were taken over by the government and the Church went underground or was wiped out by the Communist onslought. No one really knows the real position of the Church behind the bamboo curtain. There are speculations that there might be a separate, independent OMS Holiness Church in functioning in mainland China. The Society is quite confident before the Lord that a time will came when China will be opened again for the Gospel and re-entered by the OMS,

The advance of Communism in Asia, the end of colonialism, and the emergence of nationalism in Afroasian and Latin American countries posed a great threat to missionary enterprise for all the missions and denominations in these countries. But, God in His divine providence opened new avenues and new doors of opportunities for the furtherance of the Gospel. More and more countries were entered by OMS : India in 1941, Colombia in 1943, Greece in 1947. Brazil in 1950, Taiwan in 1950, Ecuador in 1952, Hong Kong in 1954, Haiti in 1958, Indonesia in 1971, and Spain in 1973. There are yet many more lands to be possessed in years to come.

4. The Policies and Strategies of the Mission

The founder and his followers were such great men of God and men of prayer that they always strove to act according to the dictates of the Holy Spirit. No country was entered without getting a green signal from the Lord. No missionary or national was appointed unless he saw clear indications of a Spirit-filled life. Dr. Wesley Duewel (1970:1) makes this very clear in his paper on "The Spirit's Ministry Through the OMS."

A study of the history of the OMS shows the continuing ministry of the Holy Spirit beginning when he called the Society into existence, through His call to its founders, and down through the years in the manifold activities of the Society. Wherever there has been missionary strategy and statesmanship during these years, it has been due to the leadership and guidance of the Holy Spirit. The continuous supply of all the needs of this growing faith organization in its world-wide outreach has been due to the faithfulness of the Holy Spirit in His providential supply, preservation, and lordship. Whenever, there has been salvation of souls and the establishment of national churches, it has been due to the faithfulness of the Holy Spirit in His total office work and in His fruit-giving ministry. Wherever there has been weakness or slow progress, this failure has been due to the human frailties of the vessels God has chosen to use, i,e., failure to fully grasp the total mind of the Spirit and to constantly obey the guidance of the Spirit ; failure in the choice of priorities, failure in total consecration or appropriation of all the Spirit's ministries in our lives, personally and collectively, in our institutions and committees.

Like any organization or movement, the OMS has been consciously or unconsciously shaped and moulded in accordance with the spirit and vision of its founder. We can very well see the imprint of his thoughts and ideas in every aspect of the Mission's life. In the matter of the life of faith, the Mission strategizes and advocates faith ; for souls, for guidance, for finance, for problems, for the ministry of healing, and a conquering faith in daily life and adventure for God. In the ministry of worldwide intercession and passion for souls and for missions, the Organization has always exhibited the zeal and the enthusiam of the founder.

Charless E. Cowman realized right from the beginning that the only way to reach the national, is through the nationals. His

58

slogan was that, "Orient must be evangelised by her own sons."
India, Africa or Brazil for that matter, must be evangelized by
the sons of their own soil. To achieve this objective from the
time of the founder until the present OMS has set out to establish
Bible schools to train the nationals in all the fields of its operation.
The Mission has also continued to make hard, bold plans to
evangelize the nations through direct evangelism by holding
Gospel meetings, literature distribution, crusades, team evangelism, radio evangelism, and whatever other direct methods that
might be suitable to the countries in which it serves. Medical
and social work have always been kept to a minimum. It has
also been a definite policy of the Mission not just to evangelize
and make converts, but to get the converts into groups and
establish them into local churches, striving toward the goal of
self-propagation, self-government and self-support. As a result
of this clear emphasis right from the beginning, churches in the
first two fields tackled by OMS, i.e., Japan and Korea, have
become self-supporting.

B. OMS ENTERS INDIA

When the door was closed in China for the Gospel, the door
opened in India. Dr. Erny, the ex-president of OMS, writing
in the "Missionary Standard" in 1950 burst out :

> The door is open in India today, but we cannot
> tell how soon it will close. Now is India's
> time for reaping. Subtle forces are at work,
> many ardent Hindus are pulling for all they
> are worth to make India a Hindustan, or a
> religious state . . . Shall not India's millions
> have at least one chance to hear the blessed
> Word of Life? Can we look on indifferently
> or turn a deaf ear to their cries? What we do
> we must do quickly. There is not a more needy
> mission field in the world than India. On every
> side appalling needs face this great nation.

1. The Survey

But, well over a half century before, as I have mentioned
earlier, India's great missionary need was felt by the founder
himself. India had always been dear to the heart of Rev.

Charles E. Cowman and he felt called to come to India during those early days soon after his conversion. But he was prevented by the Holy Spirit. However, the time came, when the missionaries who were put out of China after the Communist takeover, turned to India with hope and relief as the next possible field to be entered. Rev. E. L. Kilbourne, a close associate of Charles E. Cowman and the President of OMS after the founder's death arrived in India with his wife during the latter part of 1939 to make a careful survey. They stayed in India for several weeks and visited all the big and small crowded towns of India. A Methodist missionary, Rev. E. A. Seamands took them around. The Kilbournes naturally were quite moved in their spirit by seeing the teeming millions of India as sheep without a shepherd.

> Each other field in which we have worked had its special problems and difficulties, but in India, we seem to find not only all of these same difficulties but also India's peculiar brand of hellish opposition to the saving Gospel of Calvary and Pentecost. (Standard, Feb., 1940)

1. Why Allahabad ?

At the same time, Mr. Kilbourne in the same letter expressed great hopes for evangelism in India. As they were wandering around they couldn't get clear guidance from the Lord as to the place that OMS should begin its ministry. One morning while they were riding on the train enroute to Banaras to visit another mission work, Rev. Kilbourne awoke with a very strong urge of the spirit in his heart that the place where the train was then stopping, was the place God had chosen. He threw open the shutters on the window of the train, but just then the train started to pull away from the platform. He called out "What place is this?" And he was told, "This is Allahabad." When he got to Banaras he told of his strong feeling to the Acting Superintendent Pilgrim Holiness of the P. H. church, who drove him back to Allahabad. He simply drove around the streets of Allahabad and felt confirmed in his heart that this was the place of God's guidance. Allahabad is situated between Delhi and Calcutta. Later, early in 1941 the first OMS missionaries set foot on Indian soil. They were : Rev, and Mrs. Roy Davis, Rev. and Mrs. J. T. Seemands, Miss Mary Ella Taylor, Rev. and

Mrs. Wesley Duewel. Two weeks later they were joined by Dr. and Mrs. Eugene Erny to make "the nine gems" of the OMS in India. Among these, the Duewels and Ernys were appointed to open a seminary in North India and the remainder of the team to Mysore State.

While this latter group was in Bangalore studying language, just by providence they came in contact with an individual who told them about the property in Allahabad where the present seminary and headquarters are now built. They went and possessed it in the name of God. The seminary was opened in July, 1942. Though this place has been carefully chosen for a seminary program and evangelistic work, the soil is so hard and Satan has such a stronghold, that it has not been responsive to the Gospel. Except for a few preaching points, no churches have been organized yet. There has been, however, a small movement seventy miles southeast of Allahabad where property has been bought and a church established.

3. Gadag District

Approximately six months later, another seminary was opened in Gadag, Mysore State. Rev. and Mrs. Roy Davis, Rev. and Mrs. J. T. Seamands, and Miss Taylor were appointed to take care of the ministry. Since then, there has been intensive evangelistic effort around this area. The ministry in the early days was very difficult, but a new chapter has now opened and I shall quote a brief account from Rev. Roy Davis, who served in this area for more than thirty years:

> A new chapter of church growth began when the government built the Tunga Bandra Dam and irrigation project, of which the northern branch of canals was developed right in the main part of our district efforts. This had been a semi-famine area and the Kanarese farmers were unacquainted with wetland farming methods. Therefore, thosands of Telugu farmers migrated into our district. Among them were many Christians, who were happy for our evangelists and pastors to visit their homes and conduct

61

Christian worship services. The home meetings
became centres for evangelizing the camps.
The most logical converts were those who
formerly lived near sincere Christians and now
took the opportunity of accepting Christ in a
new situation where caste opposition was
reduced. (Davis, 1973)

Nine churches have been established so far with membership of
about 450.

4. Mid. India District

The third area entered by the OMS was Mid-India. The
District Headquarters is in Bhopal, a rapidly-growing industrial
city. Our work is found also in other towns and villages throughout this area. Rev. G. C. Khanna, an able Indian leader, and a
Hindu convert, headed the work. This town, since it is situated
right in the middle of India, had been chosen by the Indian
government to construct the Heavy Electrical plants. The
population of the town when OMS Entered twenty years ago was
only 70,000, but now the population has risen to 700,000. Almost
twenty, different denominations and groups have begun their work
here. Unfortunately, very littlle is being done by the existing
OMS Church to make use of this great opportunity.

At one stage, three Tamil pastors were sent to Bhopal to
plant churches among the Tamil-speaking people there. The work
was very successful and one church was organized and another
was well on the way while the then District Superintendent
brought in a unification policy to unite the Tamil-speaking
congregation and the Hindi-speaking congregation. When the
issue was forced upon the Tamil congregation, the Tamil Church
almost became independent. The pastor supported by the OMS
had to be withdrawn and was sent back to Madras. The Tamil
work was buried under the ground. Here is a clear warning of
what can happen if we impose one culture on another. It was
rather a sad story. However, the OMS has extended its ministry
in this area in about seven other places. See map on the next
page for the OMS Station in India.

62

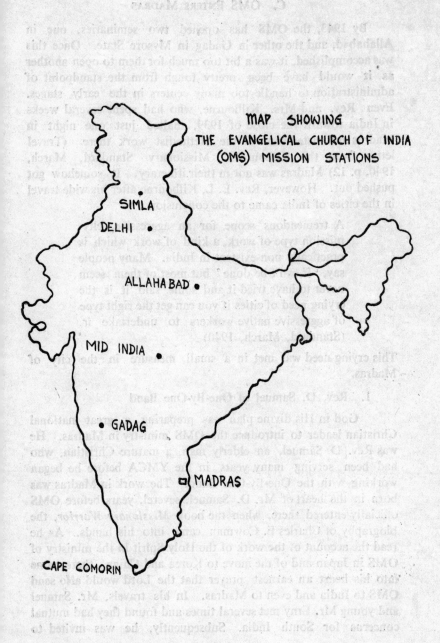

MAP SHOWING
THE EVANGELICAL CHURCH OF INDIA
(OMS) MISSION STATIONS

SIMLA

DELHI

ALLAHABAD

MID INDIA

GADAG

MADRAS

CAPE COMORIN

FIG. 4.

C. OMS ENTERS MADRAS

By 1943, the OMS has opened two seminaries, one in Allahabad, and the other in Gadag in Mysore State. Once this was accomplished, it was a bit too much for them to open another as it would have been pretty tough from the standpoint of administration to handle too many centers in the early stages. Even Rev. and Mrs. Kilbourne, who had spent several weeks in India toward the close of 1939, halted just one night in Madras and visted some of the Methodist work there. (Travel letter from the Kilbournes, Missionary Standard, March, 1940, p. 12) Madras was not in their itinerary. It somehow got pushed out. However, Rev. E. L. Kilbourne after his wide travel in the cities of India came to the conclusion :

> A tremendous scope for an aggressive, city-mission type of work, a kind of work which is practically non-existent in India. Many people say, ' It can't be done ' but most of them seem never to have tried it and some said it is the crying need of cities if you can get the right type of aggressive native workers to undertake it. (Standard, March, 1940)

This crying need was met in a small measure in the city of Madras.

1. Rev. D. Samuel of One-By-One Band

God in His divine plan was preparing a great national Christian leader to introduce the OMS ministry in Madras. He was Rev. D. Samuel, an elderly man, a mature Christian, who had been serving many years in the YMCA before he began working with the One-By-One Band. The work in Madras was born in the heart of Mr. D. Samuel, severel, years before OMS officially entered there, when the book *Missionary Warrior*, the biography of Charles E. Cowman came into his hands. As he read the account of the work of the Holy Spirit in the ministry of OMS in Japan and of the move to Korea and China, there came into his heart an earnest prayer that the Lord would also send OMS to India and even to Madras. In his travels, Mr. Samuel and young Mr. Erny met several times and found they had mutual concerns for South India. Subsequently, he was invited to

Allahabad as one of the speakers at the Spiritual Life Convention. Through these contacts, Mr. Samuel and Mr. Erny began making plans for work in Madras.

2. The Tamil Revival Magazine "Uyir Meetchi"

As a first step toward the beginning of the ministry in Madras, a Revival Magazine in the Tamil language known as "Uyir Meetchi" was introduced in 1950. The OMS had already established this magazine ministry in four other Indian languages, including English. Rev. D. Samuel became the editor, and one Mr. M. D. Enock, a retired government servant, became the manager and Rev. P. Devabuktie, from the Dohnavur Fellowship was appointed as the teavelling agent. Several hundred Christians all over Tamilnadu became subscribers to this magazine. A foundation was laid for the beginning of the ministry of OMS in Madras.

3. Bible Study Group

Meanwhile, Rev. D. Samuel began a small Bible study group in his own residence. This group met on Wednesday evenings. The class grew and grew, and were extended to Friday nights also. Rev. D. Samuel was a man of great spiritual depth. His Bible study classes were greatly appreciated by the Christians all over India. His decision to settle in Madras and to open the Night Bible School was welcomed by the Christian churches. More than fifty members were enrolled for the Bible classes. Rev. D. Samuel eventually felt compelled of the spirit to convert the Night Bible School into a regular Bible Seminary.

4. Dr. Erny's Revival Meetings at Madras Bible League

Just at this time, Mr. Erny, the then principal of Allahabad Bible Seminary and OMS Director in India was invited by the Madras Bible League. This league came into existence as a result of revival in the Zion Church at Chintatripet about which Dr. Edwin Orr mentions in his book *Evangelical Awakenings in India* The revival which began in 1905, was repeated several times down the years and a group of laymen who had accepted the Lord founded this organization known as The Madras Bible League. These men and women met every Sunday after their worship services at about eleven o'clock in the morning at the Satyanathan Memorial Hall of the Zion Church. The meeting would go on until two o'clock in the afternoon and then the believers would divide themselves into two or three groups and have open-air meetings in two or three places in the city. This tradition and practice is carried on even to this day. The Bible League also played an important part in going out with us for open-air meetings and helping us with our evangelistic programs in the early days about which I will be mentioning later.

This group invited Dr. Enry to minister in their midst in 1951. Dr. Erny and Mr. French, who came with him, were used of the Lord greatly. The late Mr. I. Joseph who had been the President of the Bible League used to tell me often:

> Dr. Erny's revival meetings made a great impact
> on my life: it was through his sermons I realiz-
> ed the great difference between doing God's
> work with our own strength and the strength of
> the Holy Spirit,

It was during these meetings that Rev. D. Samuel and Dr. Erny met and finalized their plan to open the Madras Bible Seminary.

5. Madras Bible Seminary opened

To open and establish an institution is not an easy task. The preliminary plans were underway. Mr. Victor Joseph, the first Tamilian evangelist who went to Allahabad to receive his training had returned. Yet, they didn't get started on the opening of the seminary. An American visitor, Dr. Jack Shuler, a good friend of OMS, after visiting Madras wrote in the Missionary Standard and aroused popular enthusiasm and support in America for opening of the seminary in Madras.

> The city of Madras is calling for a Bible
> Seminary for the Tamil-speaking young people
> of that great southland. This school had
> already been delayed over two years and our
> Indian bretheren working there have grown

66

discourage with our seeming indifference to this great and challenging need. (Nov.. 1952).

The challenge was taken up by the OMS Board and Rev. and Mrs. Phillippe were asked by the Mission to go to Madras and rent a suitable building to open the Bible School. The Phillippes were for many years missionaries in China until the Communist takeover. In 1946, they first came to India to serve in the place of Dr. Erny who was on furlough from the Allahabad area. Early in 1953, the Board asked them to move to Madras with plans to open the seminary by July 1953.

First they rented a building at Vepery. Since the building was not suitable, they were about to renovate it to provide more space. Just then, they received information about another compound which was available for sale. Mr. Phillippe approached the owner about the possibility of renting the property. After a great deal of persuasion, the owner agreed for what Rev. G. Phillippe calls, " a water-tight contract to rent the property strictly for one year and then at the end of the year, we must go through with the purchase or move out." This remarkable instance of God's guidance gave the OMS confidence that the seminary was in God's will.

On June 29, 1953, they moved into the building and on July 3, 1953, the Madras Bible Seminary was opened with a ceremony is which Rev. W. Khurt of Strict Baptist Mission spoke. Rev. G. Phillippe became the first Principal with Rev. D. Samuel as the Dean and Rev. E. Victor Joseph as the member of the staff. About twenty-two students were enrolled including some of the students of Rev. D. Samuel's night Bible School who became full-time students. Mrs. Elma Phillippe wrote in the Oct. 1953 issue of the Missionary Standard :

> The Madras Bible Seminary is launched
> Temporary quarters provided ... nucleus of
> students already in the dorm...new school
> welcomed by other groups ... going forward
> in dependence upon God.

CHAPTER V——IN SEARCH OF AN EFFECTIVE
CHURCH PLANTING PATTERN—(1953—1957)

At the opening ceremony of the Madras Bible Seminary on July 9, 1953, Rev. G. Phillippe announced to friends from the different churches and denominations assembled there that the purpose of the opening of the seminary was to train Tamil-speaking nationals to evagelize Tamilnadu. This was greatly welcomed by the evangelical-minded people and paved the way for a united effort to bring the city of Madras under the sound of the Gospel.

A. CHRIST FOR MADRAS CRUSADE

While the Phillippes were in Allahabad, they gained experience in distributing Gospel and tracts in a door-to-door campaign called " Christ for Allahabad Crusade." As more people are literate in cities than in villages, they felt distributing the written pages of God's Word would be an effective presentation of the Gospel.

Consequently, arriving in Madras, Mr. Phillippe organized a similar campaign. Under his chairmanship, a committee with representatives from several denominations including CSI was formed ; funds were raised and a systematic program of distributing the gospel portions began. The students of the Madras Bible Seminary played an important part in the work ; several evangelistic-minded volunteers from other denominations also joined hands in the crusade. A small section of the city was "saturated" with Christian literature. Thousands of Gospels were distributed and much money spent. Many enquires enrolled in the correspondence course.

But that was the end of it. No record shows that these enquirers were ever followed up, converted, baptized and incorporated in groups and churches. Church multiplication simply wasn't the plan and strategy of Christ for Madras Crusade. Its leaders did not expect to do that. Yet, the Word of God was sown with all sincerity.

Do we not witness this scene even today in the missionary world where many sincere men are vigorously sowing the seed, not expecting it to sprout and grow ? This too often happens in joint enterprises for spreading of the Gospel. If one of the participants in a joint effort plants new churches, he will be accused of taking undue advantage fromthe " deal, " trying to draw selfish benefit out of the " contract."

These early experiences slowly pushed the Faculty of the Madras Bible Seminary out of this general, vague seed-sowing evangelism. Meanwhile the search for an effective church planting ministry continued. Satan was busy too, Rev. Phillippe all of a sudden fell seriously ill.

B. DR RIGBY ENTERS THE SCENE

Strange are the ways of God. He chose and prepared a man, Dr. David J. Rigby, a medical doctor from Great Britain, and in 1949 sent him to British Guiana to get trained there to take up the ministry in Madras ! The Rigbys after serving a term in British Guiana received an emergency note early in 1954 from the OMS Headquarters that they should immediately proceed to India to take the place of Mr. Phillippe. The immediate reaction of the Rigbys was to say no to the request since they had always felt that they were called to serve in South America and had just organized a Bible School there. They informed the Board that it was impossible for them to leave British Guiana. Their letter, however, crossed an urgent request to cable their reply as the situation in Madras was desperate. Refferring to his struggle and God's green signal at this crucial time, Dr. Rigby writes :

> This took me again to my knees where the
> Lord broke me at His feet and showed me the
> reason I would not go to India was because of
> public opinion who would question my call.
> I told the Lord that if He would assure me this
> was His will, I would go. Immediately came

69

the reply in the Scripture of Exodus 3 : 12,
'Certainly I will be with thee.' We cabled
Headquarters and within three weeks were on
our way to Madras.

What happened in Madras the ensuing years
was to a great extent dependent on what the
Lord had already done in our lives before
we went there. (Rigby, Correspondence)

The Rigbys arrived in Madras in February, 1954, and the
Phillippes left toward the close of the same year. In 1955,
Dr. Rigby took complete charge of the seminary and the evange-
listic work.

C. YOUTH FOR CHRIST AND " GOD CALLS THE CHURCH "

South India was different to British Guiana, so Dr. Rigby
set to work reading about what others had done. He, being a
good speaker, received many invitations to speak for various
groups and churches in the city. This gave the OMS wide
contact with the other existing denominations. Dr. Rigby was
elected to the Youth For Christ Committee and became instru-
mental in the formation of this interdenominational body which
under the able leadership of Mr. Victor Manoharam has done a
tremendous work among the youth in the cities of Tamilnadu and
India. It is probable that as time goes by, even interdenominational groups such as Youth For Christ will also catch the
vision for mobilizing the youth to church planting among responsive segments of India's peoples.

Dr. Rigby along with Mr. Manoharam, Mr. Khurt of the
Strict Baptist Mission and other Chrtstian leaders in the city also
organized " God Calls The Church Crusade " to promote revival
among the churches in Madras. The program went well for a
few years. Under its auspicies, several gospel and revival com-
paigns were held. Eminent evangelists like Billy Graham, Akbar
Haq and Everett Cattel spoke at convention meetings. During
the January, 1956 Graham meetings, hundreds came forward to

accept Christ. Though these were encouraging developments, alert Dr. Rigby was looking for better opportunities and a more solid and lasting ministry in the city.

D. VYASARPADI TRIED OUT

Vyasarpädi is a settlement in which live men of many castes about six miles north of and headquarters at Kilpauk. Evangelistic work was begun by Rev. E. Victor Joseph in this area a year before the Seminary was opened. Mr. Joseph had a few paid evangelists and Bible women to help carry out the spreading of the Gospel. The mission bought a piece of land in Vyasarpadi and built a small *mat-shed* church (bamboos, and coconut thatch building). Mr. Joseph, being a teacher in the seminary, utilized the services of the students. Between 1954 and 1955, the students, I among them, were going there regularly on Sundays and after the worship service would join the paid evangelists and the Bible women in distributing tracts and preaching in open-air meetings.

Dr. Rigby finally decided to reinforce the efforts of Rev. E. Victor Joseph and his church in this area. A two-week campaign was programmed. Special speakers like Mr. Victor Manoharam were invited. The Seminary students camped in Vyasarpadi and an all-out effort was made. A few Hiudus were converted, mostly through the contact of Rev. Victor Joseph. We thought this would strengthen the church. But a strange thing happened. The few converts who had been attending the church. felt very much out of place since they were always outnumbered by the evangelists, Bible women and students who — with the best of intentions — were somewhat like " paid attendants." There was no oneness of the spirit. The converts had seemed strong in their conviction and Rev. Victor Joseph had done a considerable work among them in winning them to the Lord. But the converts found themselves in a church which was not theirs. They had to do nothing to support it. The land had already been bought and the building built long before. The church was filled with hired evangelists and Bible women and the stipendiary students. There was no necessity for the converts to take any initiative.

71

This kind of a church had not really been the intention of Mr. Joseph, but in those early days, he and Mission had no other alternative but to start some kind of a church. As months went by, the mat-shed church began to collapse. The congregation invaded the Mission Compound to appeal to the missionary for funds to fix the roof. But they were quite "disappointed" by Dr. Rigby who instead gave them the ultimatum that if they did not get together to fix the church during the time limit given to them, the property would be sold and the church shifted to some other location. The congregation did not rise to the challenge.

Meanwhile, CSI made complaints that the OMS was hiring their members and taking them away from the church. There is nothing wrong in hiring evangelists as long as there is proper supervision and a clear strategy for such workers. For all these reasons, Dr. Rigby determined to do away with all hired evangelists and Bible women. The land was sold and the church shifted to a rented hall about two miles away in Erukkamanagar where most of these converts lived. This move was a face-saving maneuver as far as the relationship of the OMS with other denominations was concerned. Further, it helped the converts to work out their own destiny. The present pastor of the church, Rev. V. S. D. Gnanadoss reported in 1972 :

> Several seminary student camps were held in this area from time to time . . . There are about sixty-six baptized members. A piece of land had been bought . . . Rev. Jeevavaran, Rev. Edward, Rev. Victor Joseph, Pastor Pandian, Pastor Henry, Pastor Moni, Rev. Daniel have served with this congregation. During the time of their ministry, a permanent church building has been built. (Gnanadoss : 1972)

These were, of course, latter developments. In 1956, we had yet to evolve an effective church planting pattern.

E. THE EVOLUTION OF " THE MADRAS PLAN "

One duty was very clear to the Faculty ; they had to train the seminary students in effective fieldwork.

1. The Way opened

" In time, I came into contact with Rev. John Piet of the North Arcot Mission " says Dr. Rigby, " who had published a small book on *Leaflet Evangelism*," (Review by Rigby) Mr. Piet shared with Dr. Rigby how he had paid men to circulate seriated tracts through a number of villages and found them to be very useful in spreading God's word. Mr. Piet also maintained a chart of various responses, using the gospel sales as an index. Then, into the most responsive areas, he would send gospel teams to evangelize, with excellent results through the villages of North Arcot.

" This plan caught fire in my soul and I felt here was something we could do with our seminary students every week-end " wrote Dr. Rigby. To do " something " with the students was the rationale in the thinking of the Faculty which led them step by step in achieving something for the Lord.

These seriated tracts were quite different from the ones which had been used by the Christ for Madras Crusade which had distributed Gospels and tracts in rather limited sections of the city. A larger section of the city, west of the railway line — the great growing edge — had no churches at all and hence could not be " reached for the Gospel " easily by the churches which had joined the Christ for Madras Crusade. Dr. Rigby states :

> This [untouched fields in Madras City] sent
> me out to survey this whole area and I knew
> we had found our 'Mission Field' which we
> could invade with the Gospel. (Ibid.)

2. On Clearing the Objective

" The world is my parish " said John Wesley. But it is a pity that we Christians have created our own little mission worlds all over the place and do not let anyone else come near. This was our constant worry in those early days. We had to be very cautious over entering into an area lest we enter into " somebody else's territory." In a large city like Madras, it is very hard to fix boundaries. There would be always a congregation here and a group there who might not have much in the form of a church and cared nothing about evangelizing "their" area; but would protest loudly if another missionary body would evangelize that section. This dog-in-the-manger mentality marked Madras City as a whole and troubled us greatly.

Church planting in India's cities and villages is constantly thwarted by this outmoded idea of comity. Many denominations and congregations claim whole cities or sections of cities. They do nothing there to plant churches but scream in outrage when anyone else does. Satan used these obstacles for some years to dissuade us from carrying out the proper New Testament type of ministry.

For us, who by not planting churches were enjoying a cordial relationship with older denominations, it was rather painful to contemplate their anger if we should break into church planting.

The leaders of the OMS also differed among themselves as to whether students were to carry on fieldwork only on Saturday evenings or on Sundays as well. Strong opinions were held, since being out all day Sunday in the field meant no opportunity for worship, which Christians ought to have, and students in other seminaries always got. Dr. Rigby, however, was firm on this. He thought a day better spent in preaching God's Word than in an hour of worship and ten hours of idle conversation. A compromise was made by having early morning worship at the seminary at 6-00 A.M., after which all students were out evangelizing.

Faculty members also differed as to what method of evangelization should be used. Should we go quietly around distributing tracts and making personal contacts? To Rev. D. Samuel, a one-by-one-band man, this appealed most. This silent ministry would disturb no one and arouse no opposition from the community. Dr. Rigby favored both methods, whether distribution of tracts and personal contacts, or open-air preaching and campaigns. He felt there wasn't time enough to sit and argue about it. He told us to go ahead and put the program into action.

3. The Strategy

The plan which gradually evolved was as follows: We would tackle one area for ten weeks (the regular academic term for the Seminary consisted of eleven weeks). Every Saturday and Sunday the student team "invaded" an area and visited every home, leaving behind one of the ten seriated tracts. In the early weeks, the students were not to spend time talking with persons, but allow them to read one or two tracts and let the Word of God speak for itself. As weeks went by, more and more personal contacts were to be made Gospels and Bibles sold. When the team had finished the distribution, on a certain day they were to hold a street meeting in a strategic point, to be repeated as far as possible on the same spot week after week. Students who had special gifts were to work among the children. At the close of ten weeks of sowing, the students were to camp in the midst of the people and hold a series of evangelistic meetings and seek "a harvest of souls."

4. The Leaflets

The idea of a systematic and concentrated evangelism was born, as already mentioned, out of Dr. Rigby's meeting with Rev. John Piet.

Ten leaflets were gotten ready and printed. Each was complete in itself telling a gospel story, such as a miracle of healing or a parable like the prodigal son. In the first few tracts, the name Jesus did not occur until toward the end of the tract so that a non-Christian reading it would not throw away the valuable treasure of God's Word. At the bottom, every tract stated that the life story of this wonderful person, written by one of his disciples could be purchased from the young men distributing them week after week.

F. "THE MADRAS PLAN". IN ACTION—
THE BIRTH OF A FEW HOUSE CHURCHES

The fulness of time had come. Dr. Rigby, without waiting for special funds or capable national workers launched this

75

program in a step of faith with the assistance of sixteen raw hands, namely the young untrained students. The pattern which is now known as "The Madras Plan" was born.

1. West Saidapet

The first experimental area chosen was West Saidapet, the whole district west of the railway line, which the Christ for Madras Crusade had discovered to be unchurched and unevangelized. We began operating here from September, 1954. The area comprised several sections according to castes. It included the township and a suburban village. The students were divided into several team of two each. Each team concentrated on certain streets and lanes. Their ministry consisted mostly of distributing leaflets and making personal contacts. If opportunities opened, we would start Sunday Schools for children in a home or verandah or under a tree as the case might be. The larger proportion of the population was made up of a caste of weavers which we found to be somewhat responsive Many gospel portions were readily bought. Good crowds listened eagerly at the open-air meetings.

After Christmas vacation, the students were sent out for two weeks for an on-the-spot camp meeting. A home was temporarily rented to house the students. Gospel meetings were held in a tent pitched on a vacant plot for this purpose.

Many of those who had been contacted by the students were invited. Many responded. Meetings were well attended by both adults and children. But no one showed any sign of accepting Christ and becoming a Christian. However, just a couple of days before the meetings were to be closed, early one morning a fine young man, Muthu by name, came rushing to the house where we were camping and told us that he wanted to become a Christian. He went on to tell us that he had been attending our meetings very regularly with an intention to find fault, but just the night before, Christ had appeared to him in a dream and commanded " Follow Me."

It was hard for us to accept the authenticity of the story. We even had apprehensions as to whether the young man was trying to fool us. But as he went on giving the full account of

76

his dream, he began to sob and cry out for salvation. We felt that something must really have happened to him. Our camp leader, Rev. P. Devabaktie, took him aside and led him to the Lord. Muthu in the Tamil language means "pearl." He was indeed a precious pearl, the first fruit of our church planting ministry. Before the compaign came to a close, two others from the same weaver caste also made decisions. Their baptism took place at Easter, 1955.

Two of the senior students were appointed to go on weekends and take care of young converts and carry on the ministry. At that early date we used these foggy terms. What we really meant was "incorporate these new converts in a Church of Christ." As there were signs of increased rssponse in the area, another camp in West Saidapet was arranged. Dr. Rigby, reporting in the June, 1955 issue of the Missionary Standard writes:

> We are now busy in the tent campaign in Saidapet. The Lord wonderfully undertook in giving us the ground for the tent again. The owner of the land is a Hindu and while he very gladly allowed us the use of the land for the first time, he was very concerned when we wanted to come back again, as he was afraid of the effect it would have on the community. However, we prayed and the Lord touched his heart and so the tent is pitched in a very advantageous point for the whole village. Also, the Lord has continued His wonderful work in the hearts of the villagers and after this further three months of sowing the Word week by week, many are showing great interest in the Lord. Good crowds have been coming out each night to both the children's meetings and the gospel services . . . Please pray much for us we seek to find a property in this area that we can rent for one of our workers to go and live there and also use his home as a center for meetings regularly. (Rigby 1970 : 4).

Since then, several pastors have been serving the Lord in this area. Though two other churches were planted by the pastors and converts of this Church, only a few converts were brought into the Christian fold and baptized. Nevertheless, the Church grew rapidly because many businessmen who were already Christians settled in this section and threw in their lot with us and became members of the Church. Land was bought and a beautiful church has been built during these years. Today there are more than 100 full members in this Church. The growth here has been mostly transfer growth, not conversion growth.

1. West Mambalam

This place is also west of the railway line north of Saidapet. Here we met with determined opposition from a high caste community. As in Saidapet, Dr. Rigby took a leading part personally in the open-air outreach by preaching and showing filmstrips. One Sunday, however, we became concious that our crowd was divided. One-half were listening carefully as we showed the pictures of "The Life of Christ," while the other half were arguing loudly how they could break up the meeting. The Lord kept the meeting in control and we concluded with prayer. When he began to drive away, the opposing group began to yell at the missionary. "This taught me that I had to take a less prominent place," writes Dr. Rigby. (Special Review, 5)

Opposition did not end our activities, however. We completed the distribution of leaflets and sold some Gospels; but the camp was totally unproductive. No land was available for a tent, so it was planned to hold open-air witness at the same spot every night. Due to the threat of opposition, however, we felt that a regular meeting would tell the opponents where we would be each night and so invite their interruption. Thus, we moved to a different location each night, with the result of dissipating our efforts. No decisions were recorded.

We were able to return to this place again in 1961. Pastor Paul Jesupatham, a graduate of the Seminary, was appointed in this place. A house was rented and we repeated the same method in reaching out into the community. This time, two young Brahmin boys were soundly converted, mostly through the ministry of Pastor Paul Jesupapatham. A few unchurched Christians in the area also joined us and regular Sunday services were held in the house of the pastor. The two Brahmin boys underwent a severe struggle and faced great persecution from their families. After remaining Christians for more than six years, caste and family pressure forced them back to "the world." I shall deal with their case in another section.

Meanwhile, sometime in 1965, we extended our ministry to a new settlement known as Ashok Nagar about two miles from this place. God granted marvelous conversions among the Harijans-the so-called low caste community. We ran a separate church for them for a few years. It came to a point where we could not rent any place to conduct worship. So this little group was attached to our West Mambalam Church. After working ten years in a high caste community, we had won two souls and lost them. But, in a matter of three months of evangelizing in a so-called low caste responsive group, several families were converted.

But we had not learned our lesson yet, for we continued in a high caste community, attempting to build up "a respectable image" of what it means to be a Christian. Families already Christian who moved in also joined us and a church arose. We purchased a piece of land and the present Rev. M. Moni is constructing a building. He is, with his congregation, also evangelizing nearby villages, wherever he finds response to the Gospel.

3. The Macedonian Call From Arumbakkam Village

Arumbakkam is a suburban village about five miles west of the Seminary. The village has a population of about 10,000 people belonging to different castes. The Lord began working in the heart of a man through the Baptist Church in a nearby village and he was saved marellously from idol worship and pagan religion. He and his family became Christians and were baptized in the Strict Baptist Mission. He was formerly known as Ellumalai, but he took a new Christian name, John. For several years, John and his family went to the Baptist Church for worship. For generations there had been a great enmity between the village to to which John belonged and the village to which he would go for

79

worship. At one stage, the situation became so bad that there were riots and stabbing incidents and killings on both sides. John and his family decided not to go to the enemy village any longer but to worship in their own home. The Lord put a great burden in his heart to bring the people of his own village to the feet of Christ. He dreamed of a church *for his own people in his own village*. Out of such dreams, people movements arise.

He had determined to approach any Christian group which might evangelize his village. He came in contact with a Syrian Orthodox Christian who was working with him in the telephone department and shared with his vision. The very next day this friend of John brought a Syrian Orthodox Priest in a car to John's little hut. John wasn't impressed at all by the priest and his long robe. He sent them off with folded hands and simply told them : "You are not going to appeal to our people with your long robes - - somehow you are not the kind of people I am looking for. Thank you for coming."

Within a few days, John happened to come in contact with an old friend, an evangelist by the name of Arthur Paul who was studying in the Madras Bible Seminary and Mr. Arthur Paul soon brought an OMS evangelistic campaign into Arumbakkam Village. We saturated it with the gospel message. Several found Christ. They erected a small hut in front of John's home on his land.

As years went by, many families were thereby added to the Lord. Land was bought and a church built. Today, there are eighty-five full members in the church, all converts from "the world. Because the church has become overcrowded, a new land has been purchased. Eventually the Church will have to shift to this new site which provides with more opportunities for evangelism. The pastor and the laymen are laboring week after week in this new section. The present Pastor Rev. Gnanaraj reports three witnessing groups in his Church and writes, "With all these organs of our Church viz., Gospel Army, Dawn Preachers, and Youth Movement, we have excellent possibilities and opportunities to extend our ministry." He means "to multiply believers and churches." (Rev. Gnanaraj, Correspondence.)

4. Aminjikarai and Otteri Congregations Established

These are two other places where small causes for the Lord, already in orbit, were enlarged and churches established.

At Aminjikarai, a place three miles west of the Seminary, the work was begun by conducting a series of meetings in a closed Methodist Gospel Hall. Several gave their hearts to Christ, mostly nominal Christians. The Sunday worship was held in one of the bel ever's home for some time and then for many years in a mat-shed church. A permanent church building has now been built. In this area (we are not able to find out why) there his not been a real breakthrough to the Hindu community. However, through one of the ladies who has accepted Christ in this church we have been able to contact her village about fifty miles away and plant a church there. I shall relate this in more detail in another chapter.

Otteri is about two miles north of OMS Head-quarters. Our ministry there began almost the same time as at Vyasarpadi, which I mentioned earlier. Rev. D. Samuel, the first Dean of the Seminary, began evangelizing this area with hired evangelists and Bible women. A few Hindus were converted and, despite of great opposition, were baptized. A small mat-shed church was built on a rented piece of land. All of a sudden there came a big setback to the work. Rev. E. Victor Joseph who was then in charge of the work writes:

> The work was much blessed by the Lord and people came in large numbers for the services. At the same time, the adversary was also busy, and some people began giving trouble, and so we had to shift the worship to the house of Rev. D. Samuel. (Rev. Joseph, Correspondence)

Trouble makers always take advantage of a situation where we conduct the worship in a rented land or a rented home. They can very easily bring pressures through the landlord. Since Rev. D. Samuel owned his home, the services went on uninterrupted for a few years. As Rev. D. Samuel was getting old, he wanted to retire, sell his property and go to his native place. Just in time, God made available a piece of ground. On it a mat-shed church was built. Now the students of the seminary were able to enter this area. In the midst of much opposition, seventy-five converts have been so far brought to the Lord and baptized. A permanent church building has been built.

This church continues to face opposition from the RSS (*Rashtriya Seva Samaj*—a Hindu militant organization). A RSS member lives right in front of the church. A board hangs in front of his home on which he from time to time displays slogans against Christianity. In the midst of all the subtle oppositions, God's name is being glorified; more and more people of the locality are being reached with the Gospel.

CHAPTER VI — SLOW AND STEADY GROWTH
(1957-1965)

In April, 1956, the first batch of seminary students graduated.
Most of the graduates were given appointments in the newly
established churches. In some cases, graduates who had played
a vital role in the planting of certain churches were naturally
asked to take care of those congregations. Those who had showed
no initiative whatsoever when they were students were not given
charge of any church, but were dropped. Thereby, a healthy
pattern evolved in that even in a student entering into the
seminary the first year would know exactly what is expected of him
by the Faculty.

A. PASTORS' MONTHLY CONFERENCE AND FELLOWSHIP

Having been placed in a city environment, the pastors frequ.
ently ran into each other. A couple of them would meet from
time to time and share prayers and burdens with each other.
There seemed to be a natural instinct to call for a get-together
meeting once a month. In 1957, this finally developed into the
form of a regular monthly conference.

This conference is held on the last Monday of every month,
in which all the pastors gather at the Headquarters.   Since the
conference day is also a pay day, every pastor is sure to be there !
We begin the morning session with prayer and Bible study which
is followed by reading reports from the workers on the battles
fought and victories won during the month. More time is then
devoted to prayer for the items mentioned in the monthly reports.

The afternoon session is a business session in which all the
programmes of the month are discussed and certain decisions made.
The problems we face in the work are also brought up and looked
into from many angles with various solutions suggested from the
floor. Notable ideas have sprung up from discussion from time
to time and have been put into effect.

One of the highlights of the conference programme is the feed-back session on the prescribed book for the reading course required by the Mission. Every pastor is expected to read six books a year.

Going back to 1957-1958, *Church Growth and Group Conversions* by Picket, McGavran, Warnshuis, and Singh happened to be one of the books chosen for the reading course. Many of the pastors neither carefully read nor tried to grasp the people movement point of view in the book. But Dr. Rigby, not only studied the book, but took time to relate its philosophy of church growth to our situation. *Church Growth and Group Conversions* expressed this great concern ;

> Across the world today in practically every non-Occidental country, numerous people movements to Christ are going on. Some are making good progress producing strong churches. Some are limping along producing weak churches. Some have stopped. Some have even died.
>
> These movements are seldom fully understood even by the church leaders and missionaries who tend them, because they are seen in the frame work of individualistic church growth so characteristic of the West. They are, therefore, frequently unrecognized and mishandled. (1936 : 1)

Under Dr. Rigby's leadership, in our ministry in Madras, we took pains to understand how and when people movements occur and churches grow ; and, we went about producing more and more strong churches.

B. A Slow But Steady Church at CIT Nagar

The next section that spontaneously opened up was a place called CIT Nagar. This was a small township built by the City Improvement Trust, hence the name.

We began church planting evangelism there in 1957. The late Rev. G. Edward, just graduated from the Seminary, had been appointed to head the team of students. The first distribution of leaflets immediately aroused the attention of a young, ardent member of the Hindu RSS. He confronted the students asking us what we were distributing. On learning they were Christian tracts, he ordered us to leave the area saying, "There are no Christians here and never will be." One day as we persisted in distributing the leaflets, he was waiting for us with a big stick and chased us around the streets. When we tried to hold an open-air meeting he came and pulled one of the students and tore his shirt and broke our musical instruments and tambourines.

We returned to the Seminary very discouraged. The following week-end, Brother Edward met us and took us to his home. assuring us that God had given the assurance of victory and that there would be church in CIT Nagar, He further encouraged us by saying ;

> The Lord has given me an aswer regarding the
> troublemaker in the street preaching. Instead
> of one meeting, we will have two — at the two
> ends of the village. While he is breaking the
> one meeting we will continue with the other ;
> when he comes to the other, the first will
> reform !

This worked out very well, and we were somehow able to carry on with the ministry throughout the term.

When the time came for the student camp to be set up in the area again, the Lord marvellously touched the heart of a landowner and we obtained permission to erect the tent on his land. We started the meetings and crowds began to attend. The RSS young fellow came almost every night and stood outside yelling at the top of his voice. One evening he devised a new method to disturb the meeting. After a chilren's meeting, he called the children over to a sweet shop where he supplied them with sweets and told them to sit in the tent and when he gave the order they were to jump up and shout and break up the meeting. At the given signal, however, the children refused to co-operate and the man rowdily tried to interrupt the speaker. The result was he was put in a cell overnight by the Police who were patrolling that area. We didn't have any trouble from him after that. A few, non-Christians and nominal Christians accepted the Lord. Brother Edward stayed behind to take care of "the group," as we called each new church.

We would not have been able to continue the ministry if the entire community had turned against us. The RSS young man was neither an opinion leader nor an innovator in that society. He was just a stranger like everybody else in that new settlement and no one wanted to get involved in any trouble. That's why he failed to carry others with him in his attempt to chase us out of that area. Then, too, we were determined to stay.

In urbanized society in at least some areas in India today every one does what pleases his own heart. The family system and the caste system of India is slowly breaking up, Hinduism is being eroded by secularism. As we started to realize this more and more, we began to make determined efforts to disciple the responsive segments of the Madras population.

The little group of believers in CIT Nagar began to assemble in the pastor's residence at 18, Fanpet Street. In addition. Brother Edward had a natural love for children and a burden to bring them to Christ. As he gathered the children of the community, the little group grew and today those children are the strong members of the church. One of the young men from this church has recently been elected to the Administrative Committee of the District.

One big hurdle in this area was that we were not able to secure land in time to put up a church building. When we began the work in 1957, the cost of land per ground was only Rs. 2,000. (A ground is 60 × 40. or 2,400 sq. ft.) The local congregation did not have the money because it had just been formed. It wasn't the policy of the Mission at the early date to lend money to any beginning church. Five years later, the congregation raised about Rs. 3,600, but by then the cost of land had gone up to Rs. 7,500. Since the members of the congregation earned mostly very low income, they were not able to build up a fund to purchase land. The cost of living during the last decade rose by leaps and bounds. By 1968, when the congregation had accumulated Rs. 9,000 the cost of the land had risen to Rs. 25,000 per ground.

Meanwhile the pastor was transferred and his house was not available for worship any longer. The believers temporarily shifted their worship to a YMCA Chapel nearby. At last some funds were made available to the local church and a land was bought. Brother Henry, a fine young man and a graduate of the Madras Bible Seminary, took charge of the congregation and laid the foundation for a permanent church building. This building is now completed through the efforts of another young pastor who succeeded him. The communicant membership of this church is about seventy-five. This church is well on the way to self-support.

The CIT Nagar Church had a number of valuable converts, One of them was Gnanadoss, who came as a non-Christian young man from a far-off village looking for a job. After accepting Christ, Gnanadoss resigned his job and joined as a student in the Seminary. He is now an ordained minister. Brother Gnanadoss has a great passion for souls and loves to work among non-Christians. He was one of those who was responsible for people movements back in his own village, which I shall mention later.

C. A CHURCH BETWEEN TWO FIRES— THE KILPAUK CONGREGATION

As the planting of churches in the city became more and more a possibility, we didn't bother about travelling eight or ten miles to find suitable place to start. We began looking for fields around the seminary. Within half a mile we found another settlement like CIT Nagar, which also had an old village nearby.

A house-to-house leafflet programme was instituted and open-air meetings held. We met with more serious opposition to the Gospel here than at any other place. Dr. Rigby remembers what happened in one of those evening meetings :

> One night I was out with the team when a
> group of non-Christians came and objected to
> our services and demanded we stop immediate-
> ly. They accused the students of being in my
> employ and refused to allow them to preach
> any further. (Rigby : A Special Review, 6)

To keep the opponents out of our sight, we decided to rent a private piece of land and hold meetings. We still continued to have trouble. However, in the midst of all this, God did a work among the people of a certain section of the community and five or six families were baptized.

Rev. K. C. Jesudasan, a pious and keen personal worker, first served here. He was followed by Rev. P. Devabuktie. I was in charge of this church from 1963 to 1969 while simultaneously teaching in the Seminary. In May, 1963, we bought the land which we had been renting for well over five years. As we got started with the church building, the non-Christians got together and began building a shrine just in front of the church where there was a small piece of government land beside the adjoining road. We did our level best to get a stay order from the Government to have the shrine removed, but to no avail. This left us without access to the main road. We had to remodel the church building with the front facing the hostile village and the back toward the Hindu shrine--it is truly a church between two fires. We constantly have troubles from the people in this locality. Despite all of this, we were able to complete a building large enough for three hundred seats.

It took three years to finish the building, mostly through the effort of a keen lay leader of our church, Mr. A. Devakadatcham, an engineer and contractor, who had also been the secretary of the church board for about six years. He had to leave our church in later years on doctrinal grounds, but ever since he left us the Lord has used him in planting churches in his wife's native village. More than one hundred non-Christians believed and were baptized. Four churches have been established so far. We look forward that the Lord will open a way in the future to work in cooperation with a man like Mr. Devakadatcham for a wider church planting ministry in India.

88

D. People Movement in Porur Village A Turning Point

Porur is one of the suburban villages between St. Thomas Mount and Poonamalle, twelve miles southwest of the Bible Seminary. It was my privilege to pioneer the work here. Porur became a turning point in our ministry, opening up the possibilities for people movements wherever we went. Porur was also a turning point in my own life by way of total commitment to God's call and understanding His plan and purpose in my ministry for Him.**

Though this suburban village was part of the City of Madras, the village had been there long before the city came into existence. The city life and the modern education had made no impact on the villagers. Every night for about six months a group of villagers would get together for a little practice for *Kuthu* - - a folk dance related to one of the stories of the deities they worship. On the final day after six or seven months of training they would stage a *Kuthu*. I saw here an opportunity to make use of the students in training them to stage a Christian drama. This worked out very well. What took six month's training for the other group took only two months for us and our performance was appreciated far better than the other group. The following year a few young men from the Kuthu group joined us and together we staged the story of the prodigal son. Hundreds of people came from other villages. Since then the Christian drama channeled and geared toward the conversion of people became a "functional substitute" for the villagers, who loved to act and dance.

Every night after school we had a time of prayer. It was amazing to see these young Hindu men praying to God and praising Him in their own words. The movement continued to spread with some of the wives accepting Christ. We did well to delay baptism until we got the group as families so that they could stand together as a church after baptism.

We had the joy of baptizing the first twelve converts in a Hindu temple tank. It was in this tank the villagers would take

---

** Readers may kindly go back to the Introduction for my personal experience in detail as it bore upon the work in Porur.

89

a "holy bath" before they went to the temple to worship and it was in this temple they now took a stand for Christ.

This kind of act and the movement undoubtedly met with opposition from the so-called high caste community. But two-thirds of the population were Harijans and since we took this entire community with us, the high caste people could do nothing against us. I still continued to m intain a friendly attitude toward people of all castes while concentrating upon the Harijans.

In June, 1960, I left for Allahabad Bible Seminary B.Th. studies. Since then, Pastors Pandian, P. M. Daniel, K. C. Jesudasan have labored in the village. As a result of their coutinued hard work and the pursuit of principles I followed in identifying with the responsive community, we have had marvellous people movements. Between eighty and ninety have been baptized so far. Land was acquired free of cost, and a place of worship built during these years.

I shall always thank God for those valuable years of revie-wing my call and the vision and challenge He placed in my heart for the ministry of discipling people for Christ. The Lord also enabled us to recognize the great potential within the masses and classes with whom He had always identified Himself. When one discovers that power of the Gospel work even today in the hearts of the people and begins to enjoy the fruit of his labor, all the sufferings and mental agony he undergoes vanishes away. I killed three snakes in the house which I occupied; I took ill often, yet the Lord delivered me. The young converts became my "devout friends," and were prepared to suffer together with me.

At Porur, the Lord gave us the greatest insight into our work and showed the vision of a responsive community. Though we recongnized this, yet we failed to make an all-out thrust to concentrate on this particular community, simply because some of the missionaries didn't want to associate our Christian activities "too much" with the low-caste group. In spite of all this, we continued to have more and more converts from the Harijans.

The Harijans are mostly hard-working peasants and cultivate the land of the rich high caste for very mean wages. In some parts of Tamil Nadu possible loss of jobs threatens those who

90

become Christians. This, however, is not true in the suburbs of Madras where the city provides them with plenty of job opportunities in one form or another. This is also becoming more of a pattern across India. With the caste system breaking down, one doesn't have to stick to his caste duties. The times are changing.

In Porur, the boys who were baptized twelve years ago are today employed in factories and in government offices. Socially and economically, they have achieved better status. If I were to go today and stand along with them, there would be no mark of difference between me and them.

There is a tremendous need these days to present the unchanging Christ to the everchanging world and di·ciple every kindred and every tongue who are responsive to the Good News.

E. A GROWING CHURCH AT "INDIA'S HOLLYWOOD"

Kodambakkam is about five miles southwest of the Seminary. Our ministry was extended to this area almost the same time as at Porur. Within Kodambakkam there are different settlements like Vadapalani. Pullioor, and Trustpuram. Our Church is situated right now in Trustpuram though we have Christian families coming from all sections of all classes of people.

The place is quite famous and well known all over the country as " India's Hollywood " because it is the second largest film-producing center in India with more than nineteen studios and many other factories connected with the film industry. Many film stars live in the vicinity. Hence, it is commonly known as satan's stronghold.

Brother Aruldoss, a convert and a graduate of the Seminary was appointed there after his graduation in 1958. A year b fore that, someone else had been doing evangelistic work there but had to be dismissed on moral grounds. Hence, when Aruldoss was appointed, there was no " group. " Aruldoss shifted activities to another section of Kodambakkam. The students were sent out and a regular literature campaign began. Brother Aruldoss is gifted with healing and casting out the demons. The Lord used this greatly and we had a good harvest of souls. Dr. Rigby recalls the time when the first baptism took place :

91

I will never forget the first baptisms here. Aruldoss had the joy of leading several to the Lord and the baptisms took place in the tank in the mIddle of the village. Hindus all crowded around and watched and quite a tension grew in the atmosphere. Aruldoss boldly preached and explained what baptism meant and then the baptism took place. To our surprise, the crowd burst into applause at the close and clapped loudly. (Special Review: 6)

Brother Aruldoss had to leave the work since he was under obligation to the National Missionary Society who had originally sent him to Seminary. This was a great setback to the work. Some of the believers were scattered. The students were unable to handle the situation.

Just at this time, Brother Sadhusingh who was ministering in the northern tip of Madras City was transferred here and was asked to establish the work. Brother Sadhusingh is a keen worker with ability to get things accomplished. He worked with the Salvation Army for awhile, took two years of Seminary training, and then enrolled in the Madras Bible Seminary. He graduated in 1958, and took charge of Trustpuram Church in 1959.

His previous background and experience placed him in a good position with people. The Lord used him and his wife to lib rate many families. Things began to fall in line. A small group of converts began to assemble in his home. As the little church increased, a mat-shed building for worship was erected by the side of his rented home. The students helped out on week-ends. Evangelistic campaigns were carried on.

Brother Sadhusingh and his wife systematically visited the homes of all the people living in that locality. As both husband and wife are quick to make friends and influence people, many families began to attend the hut church Every month new converts were "added to the Lord." Since it was difficult for the pastor to take the baptismal candidates month after month to a far-off lake or river, he built a baptistry beside the church. Week after week the church grew stronger.

When Sandhusingh was transferred from Trustpurm to Saidapet, we found the house where he was living was not going to be rented to us any more. Sadhusingh had only a few weeks before he had to hand over charge of the church to Rev. G. Edward who was succeeding him. But the Lord worked miracles. A piece of land was put up for sale by a widow for a very low price. The Mission bought the land immediately and a semi-permanent church was built in a matter of two weeks and Sadhusingh was able to leave the church with a sense of a task well done.

The Lord has been putting His seal and approval on our ministry from time to time. When the circumstances threatened us and the churches (stations, we called them) were almost to be closed, God who cares for His " little flock " always intervened and placed us in a better position than before. House churches and worship places on rent d land always involves disadvantages. Most little churches face many uncertainties. But when the Lord opens a way out of such situations, it always brings joy to the heart of the young converts.

When Rev. G. Edward took charge, he filled the church with children as he had done in his previous church. He also systematically built up the congregation in giving according to God's Word. Today this church, tops the list for tithes, offerings of all our other churches. Rev. G. Edward suddenly went to be with the Lord on Good Friday, 1968.

I temporarily shepherded the church for a few months. Pastor Henry, a calm and persuasive worker succeeded me and the church is growing more and more strong under his able leadership. The full membership of the church is 175 of which 85 per cent are first generation Christians. What a joy it is to see such a multitude being discipled from the world.

F. The Call of the City Reaffirmed

As churches began to sprout slowly in all directions, the OMS began to turn its attention to Madras. Ever since it had lost properties worth millions of dollars in China, when it had to pull out at the Communist takeover, the Mission authorities were careful about buying property in other parts of Asia. However, when they began to hear the remarkable stories of how seminary students had gone about planting churches all over the city of

Madras, they sensed in this God's call, and decided to purchase the seminary property which we had been only renting until 1960, as a first step toward consolidating the work. Rev. Rudolf M. Rabe, who was Principal of the Seminary, mentions reasons which led to the purchase of the property :

> It was this very response in South Asia's most Christian city that has led to the decision to purchase prop.rty for the Madras Bible Semi nary where an effective programme of training young Tamil Christian men can be carried on. (Missionary Standard, Nov., 1960 : 4)

This meant that the Oriental Missionary Society had been testing Madras City and had found it responsive to the Gospel and had decided to stay. Mr. Rabe wrote an article in the Missionary Standard, "The Call of the City," giving the rationale for our presence in India's third largest city. It is so significant in understanding the policies which govern OMS work that despite its length, I quote from it extensively :

> .. Many others, too, in modern india are hearing the call of the city and are finding their way into the metropolitan areas despite the large population already amassed there. It is altogether possible that there will be a hundred lined up applying for the same job, and there will be very little prospect of finding suitable living quarters since the city housing programme already lags far behind the bulging population. But still there is a far greater opportunity to make one's way in the city than ever could be found in the dusty, decaying village ..

> In the south, Madras, India's third largest city, is unmistakably calling to us. The Gospel is no new thing in Madras...

> The presence of so much Christianity has led some to say to more recently arrived missionaries, 'You've come thirty or fifty years too late! Things aren't nearly so pagan as they used to be, you know. Now there are plenty

94

of churches and a good number of Christians to carry on Gospel work. Why not move on somewhere else ?'

Move on ? But the city and its needs still call so loudly. Eighty thousand Christians ? Perhaps, but how about the 1,800,000 others who are cramming the streets and bursting the seams of Madras ? Many churches already ? Yes, but how about the large residential areas where there is only a mosque or a temple ? Many missions already at work ? Undoubtedly, but too frequently it is merely caring for the "flock" which increases by natural procreation instead of from an effective programme of Gospel propagation aimed at the unevaugelized.

Establishing a new church in the city situation is not without its problems (unavailability of land, or if available, exorbitant prices which a small, poor congregation finds exceedingly difficult to raise), but there are wonderful opportunities which cannot be duplicated in a village situation. The very concentration of population makes it easy to reach the masses with the Gospel, and the people the more potential congregations there are. Further, this mass of humanity acts as a sort of " protective cover " for those who find the courage to break away from the past and turn to a new group for religious fellowship. In the city where an individual is just one among thousands of others, it is easier to identify oneself with the Christian community and attend a Christian Church than it would be in the village where everyone is known by everybody. The new city believers can become strengthened and established in their faith without some of the pressures of persecution that village Christians must often experience.

Many have gotten here ahead of us, but there
is still unlimited scope for advance. The cry
of the unredeemed city cannot be stifled by the
few church bells which ring; neither must it
fall upon dull insensitive ears, for surely the
Lord Jesus continues to say, 'Be not afraid...
I have much people in this city.' (Rabe,
Missionary Standard, Nov., 1960 : 4).

So then, God gave us His promise for "much people in the
city." We forged ahead expecting great things from God,
attempting great things for God.

G. Nungambakkam—A Church on a City Dump

In the hallway of an apartment building ? A church service ?
The public corridor was not conducive to worship, but the young
pastor, Devanandam, was determined to make good his appointment to the little congregation in Nungambakkam, which is about
three miles southwest of the Seminary. Devanandam graduated
from the Seminary in 1963, and was appointed as a paid member
of the evangelistic team the same year.

It was a special assignment, for Nungambakkam had been
one of the Seminary's targets in 1963. For two terms the students
had focused their efforts and prayers for this village, situated
inside the city. The densely populated area was divided into
sections by a main bazaar, which suggested a natural strategy.
For the first term, activities had been concentrated on one side—
every home was visited every week for three months- Armed
with a completely new set of individualized leaflets, the students
left one of the "Series of Twelve" each week, and began conducting five Sunday Schools for non-Christian children and several
open-air meetings. A few people showed interest.

During the next term, efforts had been directed to the other
half of the village. The same methods were used each week-end.
Then the Monday mornings, as usual, the students gathered
together at the Seminary for report and prayer.

Thus, at the end of nine months work, ten to twelve people
accepted Christ, coming from a background of non-
Christian and Christian. At the close of the school year, Devanandam, one of the graduates, was appointed to shepherd the

little flock.   He searched for land on which to put a hut, but in vain.   His only alternative was to ask the landlord of the apartment where he lived to allow a worship meeting in the corridor. Surprisingly the landlord granted permission and twenty to thirty Christians and enquiries came each week to worship and learn more about the Gospel of Jesus Christ.

A few months later as the numbers increased, the corridor became so crowed that it was more and more difficult to worship. These regular meetings and crowds of people coming to the apartment was very embarrassing to the landlord, who had not expected any such turnout.

Pastor Devanandam continued looking for a piece of land that the congregation could rent to put up a hut.   One day he happened to hear through his congregation about one of the city dumps, a large, low area used by the city corporation to dump rubbish, was being occupied "illegally" by the poor people to build huts.   The pastor and the congregation with the help of a Christian Inspector of Police of that area by the name of Mr. Peter immediately occupaied a section and erected a large hut. After all, they reasoned, heaven and earth is the Lord's,   He is the owner of all of it.   There is nothing wrong in occupying a piece of waste land to build a small place of worship for Him ! The place stank for the corporation continued to dump garbage there.   Yet, the church inside was clean and beautiful and those who worshipped there soon got used to the smell.

Three years later, when Rev. D. Sundarsingh took charge, the congregation decided to erect a permanent church building. Mr. Moni, the treasurer of the church, who is an engineer by profession gave of his talent and time in building this church. Sundarsingh, being a young man himself, worked among the youth and built them up in the Christian faith.   A beautiful church was built on the city dump.   When they were digging the foundation, they realized they had to go deep and remove all the rubbish and build the foundation on the solid rock.   This they took to be symbolic of that whole congregation, who recognized that in the midst of the "sinful and rubbish" world around them, were called to live a radiant life having laid their foundation on Jesus, the solid rock.

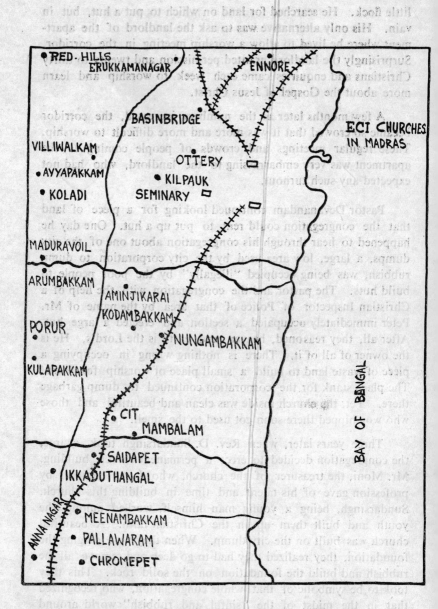

FIG. 5—Map showing the "organized" churches of ECI in the
city of Madras by 1973.

CHAPTER VII—RAPID CHURCH GROWTH
(1966—1972)

There came a time in our work where the Seminary students were not able to handle all the many centres during the week-ends. Most senior students were assigned to take charge of little congregations which did not have full-time pastors. Right at this time, the young converts receiving instructions from God's Word and growing in the Lord, spontaneously threw in their lot with the church planting programme. A pattern of evangelization emerged, remarkably like that of the New Testament.

A. Laity Mobilized : Basic Theory

A church is not an end in itself; it is rather a means to an end. "The fire exists by burning and the Church by mission," says Emil Brunner. The New Testament Church was a missionary community. Any movement that has penetrated the hearts of people and transformed lives is bound to find a way of expression. This is always evident in the early stages of the formation of the Church anywhere.

The first converts with the highly prized new gifts and achievement in Christ, are constantly looking for an opportunity to share with others. But if a convert becomes a member of a congregation where all that he is expected to do is to sit in one of the *polished pews* for one hour on Sunday and do nothing else, he will quit the church or join some other church that utilizes his talent, or else will soon quite unconsiously form opinions that being a Christian means to attend once a week, once a month, or once a year! It is tragic that some churches have developed a system that places a partition between the clergy "the anointed ones" (who do all the work) from the rest of the people (who do little except give money), while Christ has removed this partition, ending the veil from top to bottom, making us *all royal priests.*

99

The new order that He has brought for us has not been fully utilized by many churches. Christ as the first " layman " took the role of a high priest but broke the order of a Levitical psiesthood, making it null and void. The early history of the Church affords evidence of the power of the New Testament teaching that all believers are called to witness. The problems that confront some modern churches of raising a budget and hiring full-time pastors was no concern for the New Testment Church.

In the New Testament, the leadership patterns of the church were in the formative stage and were still quite flexible. The practice of one paid clergyman heading each church was not mentioned by Paul and his contemporaries. We know that some congregations met in the homes of believers in various cities. From time to time these churches were visited by traveling apostles, evangelists, prophets and teachers. (Braun 1971 : 35)

Among the first Christians, we see the entire community involved in the spreading of the Gospel. The first Indian Christian leader who remarkably succeeded in planting churches through the laymen was Bishop Azariah of :Dornakal (1874-1945). He vigorously promoted the slogan "Every Christian a witness " and considered the Church as the " divinely appointed instrument of evangelism to the world. " (Ibid. : 135)

I need not elaborate on this here. In my last chapter I shall discuss how we can use the laymen effectively in church planting. The scriptural mandate for the lay witness is clear.

B. OMS EXPERIENCE IN MADRAS : BASIC PRACTICE

In Madras, a handfull of laymen, under the leadership of the pastors, were mobilized to witness.

Our greatest advantage lay in the seminary being in the city and our churches being situated close to each other. This made it possible for us to gather the believers often for Bible study, fellowship and for united action. Each church carried on its

100

evangelistic outreach in its own capacity. The laymen got together often for sharing with one another and for Bible study at night.

Between 1965 and 1967, a young missionary, Mr. Graham Houghton, came to work in our midst. He was a creative thinker and loved to work among the youth. He was assigned to work among lay people and to mobilize them in direct evangelism. Once a month he arranged for youth rallies in the Seminary on Saturday evenings when the students were away on their own programme. The first rally had ten young men in attendance, but soon more than one hundred came. The laity were challenged time and again.

Meanwhile, Rev. John Ferris, one of the senior missionaries who had served in India more than twenty years, returned to Madras for a second term and conducted a series of Bible studies from the Book of Acts. As the interest grew among the laity (many of them recent converts) he worked out a schedule to visit all the churches and hold in each Bible study classes lasting one week. In this way, within one year he covered all the churches.

As the enthusiasm was stirred up among the congregations, the lay people began spreading the gospel message in a much more dynamic and systematic way that the students had been able so far to do. Church growth thinking constantly emphasizes that new converts and lay people are more effective in spreading the Gospel than preachers, missionaries and students. When we began to follow this principle, our churches started to grow.

C. CHURCHES PLANTED BY CHURCHES

1. Kilpauk Congregation Plants Villiwakkam Church

In the last chapter, I mentioned about the Kilpauk congregation near the Seminary. It was a church between two fires. It endured much persecution for the sake of the Gospel. But out of its suffering came the spirit of evangelism.

Every Sunday afternoon in 1966, I took some of the laymen on cycle evangelism to a *pattai** northwest of Kilpauk known as

---

* a settlement

Villiwakkam. We began systematically distributing tracts and holding open-air meetings in the old town where the high caste people lived. After several weeks of ministry, people showed no interest. We felt some uneasiness about our whole approach.

One Sunday evening, the lay leader of the Kilpauk Church, Mr. Joseph Singh, and I got on our cycles and travelled further on, exploring the locality. We soon reached a railway line, apparently the Madras-Bombay route. Beyond the railway line we found a long strip of houses that looked like a new settlement. We entered the area and handed a tract to the first man we met. He immediately responded by saying, "Sirs, I am a Christian here. My name is Peter. Where do you come from?" We told him who we were. Mr. Peter took us to his home and asked us to pray for him and his family. After prayer, we told him what we were doing on the other side of the railway line. Mr. Peter urged us to come to his side. He promised us that he and a few other unchurched Christians in the settlement would join with us in our effort to evangelize the area.

The next week we followed the guidance of the Lord and moved to this section of Villiwakkam. Mr. Peter had everything arranged for us. After the distribution of tracts, we met at one of the believer's homes to conduct Sunday School for the children. The man who opened his home for us was Mr. John Sika, an evacuee from Burma. He and his highly educated family settled in this part of the suburb because some of his family were employed in the nearby schools.

Week after week our little Sunday School built up, more and more non-Christian children began to attend. We divided the Sunday School into several sections and Mr. Sika's daughters volunteered to teach some of the classes. As this open-air Sunday School was in progress, some non-Chrstian parents and other adults began to gather around to watch what was going on. They were soon led into an evening gospel meeting at the close of the Sunday School.

This went on for several months. The Lord began to work in the hearts of the non-Christians attending the gospel meetings.

Several non-Christians accepted Christ and about nineteen belonging to six families received instruction from God's Word in preparation for baptism.

The students of the Seminary also rented a house, lived in Villiwakkam and helped in the evangelism in every way. The converts were growing in the Lord. It was a joy to see men and women who had given themselves to idolatry and uncleanness make a decision for Christ and let Him be Lord of their lives. Fifteen young discipls of Christ, belonging to a few families, were baptized on Easter Sunday, 1967. A new church was born. Many nominal Christians who were watching the lives of these young converts began attending the meetings and accepted Christ.

As the church grew, it became very crowded and not convenient to have meetings in Mr. Sika's home, particularly during the rainy season. In 1968, the Mission purchased a piece of land from the Central Fund for Rs. 8,000. This brought tremendous joy to the hearts of the new little congregation. Members joined together and built a small church (35' x 17' in size) in a matter of ten weeks. I remember very well those days how these Christians, new and old, worked day and night singing and praising God and joking with each other. Except for some parts of the masonry work, the entire church was literally built by their own hands.

They did not stop there. In the following year, 1969, since the small church could not hold the rapidly-growing congregation, they laid the foundation for a much larger building, This new building is now completed. It cost about Rs. 30,000 to complete, of which half was raised by the congregation and the other half was given by the Mission from monies sent from America by devout Christians in memory of a loved one.

Villiwakkam congregation has been an example to the other congregation in many ways. The youth of the church are known for their evangelistic zeal. Its present pastor, James Srinivasan takes these men on evangelistic outreach to the nearby village where there are possibilities of a church to be planted soon. The congregation in 1973 has a membership of over one hundred fifty people. The Lord continues to add to the Church such as are being saved.

2. Saidapet Church Branches Out to Chromepet

As I mentioned in Chapter VI, Saidapet was the first church planted by the students in the year 1956. After ten years, it gave birth to its first "baby". During 1960–1965. Rev. Moses was the pastor of the church. One Christian by the name of Devadoss who was living in the Chrompet area in the southern part of the city near Tambaram, used to visit relatives every Sunday in Saidapet, who were members of our church there. Mr. Devadoss began attending services with them. He was so impressed that he talked to the pastor and invited him to begin this kind of a church in Chrompet. The pastor surveyed the place, and started some kind of church in the house of Mr. Devadoss.

When Mr. Sadhusingh took over the Saidapet congregation, he and the laymen visited the Chrompet area often. Cottage prayer meetings were arranged in the homes of other Christian families and well wishers in the Chrompet area.

When Sadhusingh realized the great scope for church multiplication in this area, he immediately informed Rev. G. Edward and Dr. Rigby about it and volunteered to move to Chromepet if the District Administrative Committee approved.

It did, and he was transferred to Chrompet. Being a good pioneer, he visited all the houses in the area as he and his wife had done before in Trustpuram and made number of contacts. One, Mr. Jesupatham, a Christian politician and philanthropist, observing brother Sadhusingh's earnestness in trying to establish a church, came forward to donate a piece of land to the great cause. A hut church was immediately erected. The services which so far being conducted in a private nursery school, were shifted to the hut. Many aceepted the Lord and were baptized. Several Christian families who came to live in this area chose to attend the services.

Rev. P, J. Sadhusingh is a good administrator. He takes pains to maintain records and registers and appoints committees. The church at Chrompet, like most of our churches in the city, has the advantage of having qualified men capable of handling church business and running the church administration well. The pastor and the congregation put up a large, beautiful building costing about Rs. 40,000, of course, with considerable financial aid from OMS.

Brother Sadhusingh mobilized the entire congregation — both men and women — to witness for Christ. He preached a series of sermons on evangelism, challenging the hearts of the believers. Members, who were attending the church from a distance of three or four miles, organized Sunday Schools and gospel meetings in their own homes. These came to be known as out-stations.

The first one of these out-stations was organised in a new settlement of all castes known as Anna Nagar, named after the founder of the DMK party. (Anna was the founder of DMK, Nagar means city.)

Every Saturday evening, gospel meetings were conducted in the front yard of one of the Chrompet member's home. Many attended regularly and became Chrstians. The young believers got together and built a gospel hall. Regular gospel meetings are now going on Sunday evenings and an early Sunday morning worship service is also conducted for Christians not able to worship at the main Chrompet Church.

As it has happened in so many other cases in our work, a new church is now being planted as a result of one of the members of the Chrompet Church, Mr. Nathan, having to shift to his newly built house in Pallavaram, which is about four miles from the Chrompet Church. Mr. Nathan is a businessman, the manager of the Madras branch of the Alvitone Company (a baby food product). Before becoming its manager he was already a very rich man, exporting Indian-made products to Europe and other parts of the world. As his wealth is increased he went far from God. But later on due to some international cristions, he lost all his wealth and became a very dejected, losing all hope in God and religion. Under these spiritual conditions, he and his family moved to Chrompet since the Alvitone Company, which is situated near Chrompet, offered the managership of the company to him.

By God's divine plan, Mr. Nathan and his large family rented a home near the Chromepet Church. His wife and children began attending the Church. Mr. Nathan could not care less for the things of God. He thought it would be humiliating for him and for his family to attend the mat-shed church. The pastor, Rev. Sadhusingh, after much prayer visited him expressed genuine concern and love for him. Mr. Nathan finally decided to attend the church and gave his heart to Christ.

Years later when he shifted to Pallavaram, his chief concern was to open a church in that newly developing area. From the very first month, gospel meetings were conducted in his home every Sunday evening. The laymen from Chrompet and seminary students in a joint effort conducted a compaign in the summer of 1972. Since many became Christians, the Chrompet Church. which had pioneered this area, asked the Mission to purchase a plot of land. At once land was purchased from the Central Fund on condition that the new congregation assumed responsibility for putting up a small building for worship, which they did.

A church at Saidapet gave birth to church at Chrompet; Chrompet, in turn, gave birth to two other churches and is well on the way to producing more. In a matter of five years, the Saidapet Church saw "grandchildren" and is soon going to see "great grandchildren." This kind of church growth among the masses must sweep the great country of India. Rev. P. J. Sadhusing reports :

> Our total membership is 180 with a community of over 300. We have become 80 per cent self-supporting. Within one year the church hopes to come under complete self-support, We are vigorously preaching the Gospel and establishing churches in the suburbs at the radius of six or seven miles around Chrom-

pet. We, right now, have ten preaching points at Anna Nakar, Pallavaram, Royapettah, Ganapathipuram, etc. (Sadhusingh, Special Correspondence).

3. Otteri and Basin Bridge Churches Open up Ennore Church

A church is not like stagnant water, it's like a river that streams in all directions to irrigate the parched land. A tree that stops growing begins dying. So it is with church. But, praise God, that He in Madras gave rise to churches that produced churches.

I discussed the Otteri Church in Capter VI. This church in collaboration with the church at Basin Bridge has established churches along the northern border of the city. Basin Bridge is one of the first churches planted by the seminary students.

Antony, one of the early converts from Basin Bridge Church, was led to the Lord through the ministry of Rev. V. S. D. Gnanadoss. For many years he was without a job. But, in answer to prayers by the congregation he secured a job in the Government Thermal Power Station at Ennore which is about fifteen miles north of Basin Bridge and twenty miles northeast of Madras Bible Seminary. Ennore with many factories owned by the private and public sector of the country is a few miles away from the northern city limit. The Thermal Power Station was built several years ago by the State Government to provide electric power to certain part of Tamilnadu. When brother Antony got a job there he shifted with his family to Ennore. This put them in very difficult situation for attening church. However. they made it a point to attend the church at Basin Bridge at least once a month. Meanwhile, Antony looked around the area for a Protestant Church. To this surprise he could find none.

Then it dawned on Antony, "Why not start a church right in my home." He prayed about it and went to see Rev. V. S. D. Gnanadoss who was at that time in charge of both Basin Bridge and Otteri congregations.

Mr. Gnanadoss is a Hindu convert himself and is zealous for the Lord. On his own initiative, he organized a "Gospel Army." During a government holiday in 1969, Gnanadoss took his Gospel Army with him to Ennore. They spent one full day preaching the Gospel. The team found the area very open to the Gospel and decided to send two men with Gnanadoss each week-end to sow the seeds of the Gospel in the area and to conduct Sunday evening gospel meetings in brother Antony's home. At Mr. Gnanadoss' request, a couple of seminary students were also sent. Many who had become brother Antony's friends started attending the meetings. As months passed, others began coming and Antony's little home could not accommodate all of them. The service was shifted to a bigger home of a believer in the locality and then finally on to a nursery school.

One Sunday evening, Mr. Gnanadoss was returning in a bus while the other men rode their cycles. The bus in which he was travelling collied with a truck. Let me quote what he had to say here because it is a very important in connection with the work at Ennore

> Our ill-fated bus came head on in collision with a heavily-loaded truck. Both the vehicles capsized. That was all I know. I cried out 'save me, Lord Jesus.' Others cried and screamed. I somehow managed and struggled to come out. Hundreds of people came rushing to the spot. Both the drivers and fifteen others died on the spot. All the rest except me had some injury or other. I personally helped carry some of the injured persons, put them on other vehicle and took them to the hospital.

> On the way to the hospital, I counseled with these men and prayed for them, When the folks at Ennore came to know that I was the onely one spared without even a scratch on my body, they couldn't believe it. A few weeks later a young man came to my meeting and

108

came to me with tears and told me that he was
one of those I had helped carried to the
hospital and that he would like to know how
to become a Christian. Through this good
Samaritan service and the miracle that God did
with me by saving my life, I became very
popular in the locality. (Gnanadoss, Correspondence)

Even if Gnanadoss had been a medical doctor and had
been ministering to the physical needs of the people in that locality, he could not have won their hearts in several years as
completely as he did after that accident in a single day. On
principle, the OMS and the ECI never get involved in
social and medical work; however, our pastors do always serve
the sick and the needy within the congregation and extend that
service to non-Christians at the time of an emergency. No
preacher passing by would ask a drowning man whether he is
Christian, Hindu or Moslem; instead he would do the best he
could to save the life of that man. So, also, there is a place for
"service." but it has to be done in proportion.

At Ennore the work turned a corner. A student's camp
was held to consolidate early evangelistic gains. Despite strong
opposition, many accepted Christ. Land was bought and a small
mat-shed church built. The congregation has over sixty full
members. Half of them could be classified in the C^1 category.
The believers are thinking of establishing a new church and plan
to start a brick building soon.

4. Kilpauk Reaching out

When we completed our Villiwakkam Church, the congregation at Kilpauk prayed that the Lord might lead us to another
needy area where we could plant another. On the fifteenth of
May, 1968, I assembled some young men from my congregation.
The middle of May is always the hottest time of the year with
temperature goings up to 112°.

However, about ten of us — laymen, college and high
school students — left on our cycles early in the morning "in

109

search" of a new area. We had some idea as to the direction in which we should move. We had plans to cover about fifty miles that day in the hot sun. We planned to go west toward the little suburban town of Poonamallee, then move to another town called Avadi and travel toward the northeast and return home via Red Hills (see map, Fig. 5).

We made very good progress, singing and preaching all the way. Until noon, we did not come across any suburban village that spontaneously placed a challenge in our hearts. But, at about one o'clock we reached Kaduvetti. We decided to halt and eat lunch, rest for a while and then proceed. As we went into the heart of the village, there on the main road we suddenly beheld a giant idol about fifty feet high and twenty feet wide standing majestically by the road, challenging us. We stopped, wheeled our cycles into the dense shade of a big tree nearby and ate our lunch. We unanimously decided to tackle this village in the name of God. Then we rode on, but the rest of the suburban villages we visited that day were somehow an anti-climax !

The following week I went with some laymen from Kilpauk and Aminjikarai congregations to systamatically sow the seed of the Gospel in Kaduvetti. Later during the year, the seminary students also joined us and we vigorously carried on the ministry. After one year of systematic evangelism we had a summer camp in Kaduvetti with picture shows, presentations of gospel messages through slides, dramatizing the parable of the prodigal son, and much preaching and singing. With all the sincere efforts that we put in, we had not won a single convert for the Lord. We were very much disappointed because we were quite sure that the Lord was going to give us the souls and a church would be planted here.

We didn't want to quit the area because we felt the Lord had led us to that village. We therefore, determined to stay there for at least one more year. We continued to evangelize and nothing happened. There were two Christian families in that village of whom one was very helpful to us. They told us their honest opinion that the place was mostly high caste and wouldn't become Christian.

110

At the close of the second year, some of our men were preaching in a village called Ayyapakkam, three miles from Kaduvetti. There they came across a man, Moni, who had heard about Christ when he was twelve years old and since then had been secretly following Him. Mr. Moni was glad that these men came and told them that his house was open for them and they could conduct meetings there.

We paid immediate attention to this invitation and arranged to send two laymen regularly to Ayyapakkam. Two students from the seminary also went to help them. Mr. Moni invited all his relatives to attend the meetings. The front yard of his home was filled with people. After three months of ministry, we had ten days of capaign there in which the laymen and the Seminary students joined. One week later, Mr. Moni and his relatives (about eighteen of them) were baptized. Mr. Moni donated a piece of land on which to build a church. Since land cost us nothing, two-thirds of the building cost, about Rs. 3,000, was met from the Central Fund, though 50% is our regular policy. The converts raised the balance and a beautiful church was built.

After Ayyapakkam, we tackled another small village called Koladi, still set amongst the fields and brick yards gave us opportunities to witness. In a few months, twelve were baptized. Here, again, we obtained free land from the local *Panchayat* (village board). From the beginning until the present about sixty-two people have been discipled in these two villages.

The missiological significance in the these instances is quite obvious. From 4968 we have been evangelizing an unresponsive population at Kaduvetti with no results. In 1970, we turned our eyes to the fields that were with and ready for harvest. And we had a wonderful harvest, again among the suppressed class, namely the Harijans. The Lord had a purpose in leading us to that place. It is a strategic township placed on the main road, giving us access to all the villages round about. Our only interest in this big village is that it provides us with houses that we could rent for pastors that we would not be able to find in the smaller villages. Under normal conditions, we never stay in a place more than two years if we have found the soil to be unproductive. We keep ourselves on the move looking for fresh harvest fields.

111

How often in the past missionary organizations and leaders and how often the present church organizations and bishops have been sticking to unresponsive and resistant populations, for historical or sentimental reasons. They started there and feel compelled to continue.

Neither do we in our strategy in Madras build churches for any congregation. Though financial assistance is given in the form of loans and memorial gifts, this done only to the congregations who have already raised a substantial amount of money toward the project. In no case have we put up a church building hoping that the Lord would one day give us the congregation. It is a bad policy to erect a church building before there is any sign of a visible eongregation.

I shall never forget an interesting episode in the history of the Church Missionary Society back in my own native village of Pannavilai in the Tirunelveli District, four hundred fifty miles south of Madras. Rev. Thomas Tucker came to Pannavilai in the nineteenth century and built a large church building with a capacity for 3,000 people. He built this before there was even a sizeable congregation. He built the church close to the high caste Brahmin and Vellalas who were benefited by studying in the school attached to this Church and never made any profession of Christ. However, the Nadar caste people who lived little away from this church became Christians by the hundreds. The Nadars built their own churches for themselves in their respective villages. The almost empty "cathedral" built by Rev. Thomas Tucker stands as a monument to a wrong missionary strategy — without any congregation of its own except a few families who happened to be mostly high school teachers.

D. EVERY CHURCH A CHURCH PLANTER

The church growth movement that began with a few of our congregations has spread to all the others. Until 1966, we had only eleven churches. By 1972, we had thirty churches. In thirteen years, eleven churches ; in seven years ninteen churches. In 1966, the membership of the comunity was around 1,000 ; by 1972 it had increased to 5,000. It was in these years that we discoveerd the responsiveness of Harijans and began to follow

112

the contacts of the new Christians. If every church in India, big
or small would engage itself in church planting evangelism among
the present responsive population, in a matter of a quarter of a
century much of India would become Christian.

E. SODALITY AND MODALITY

Dr. Ralph D. Winter in his little book *Warp and the Woof*
discusses the need of Sodality Churches that help reproduce
membership. But his main concern is that need for modality
within sodality - - an organization like a club, or the Jesuits
within the Roman Catholic Church. Dr. Winter in another
article in the "Evangelical Mission Quarterly" says that the need
of the hour is not an emphasis on "indigenous churches" but an
indigenous mission agency.

> The concept of 'the indigenous church' is
> widely emphasized today. But how much do
> we hear about the indigenous mission agency?
> The task of church planting is important, but
> what about the art and science of mission
> planting. We study the strong and week points
> of different types of church policy. But where
> is there equivalent scholarly inquiry into the
> nature and structure of different types of mis-
> sions? We many have enough handbooks on
> how to start a church, but we have no hand-
> books at all on how to start a mission.
> (Evangelical Mission Quarterly, Summer,
> 1971)

Almost every little church of ours in Madras has: some kind
of an organization that is solely responsible for evangelistic outreach. A Gospel Army, a youth league, and ever so many other
organizations are laboring week after week planting churches.
The church at Kulapakkam near Porur and the one at Ikkadu
Thangal near Saidapet were established as a result of joint enterprise by the seminary students and the evangelistic teams from the
nearby congregations. The church at Ikkadu Thangal, two miles
southeast of Saidapet was planted mostly through the congregation
at Saidapet under the able leadership of Rev. A. Amos.

F. Summer Outreach

One other recent evangelistic campaign in which the youth organizations of the district were involved was the "Summer Outreach." Rev. D. Sundarsingh, the present pastor at Kilpauk and the Dean of Madras Bible Seminary, saw something of this sort going on in Tanjore District and felt it could be adopted for our churches also. The strategy is to take as many young men as possible to villages during the summer vacation and train them to witness and to preach in the responsive villages. This pattern is now becoming very effective and are able to plant churches through this ministry.

G. Urban Church Growth—A Key to People Movements in Villages

Mr. George Samuel, who has done extensive research among the Protestant Churches in Bombay has discovered that the church growth in Bombay is affected mostly by the immigrant Christians who have come from all parts of the country looking for jobs. Even the four hundred and five non-Christians who are reported to have been baptized between 1967–1972 are those who already accepted Christ through some Christian influence back in their own villages. Mr. Samuel reports of no case in which churches spread from the city to the villages. (Samuel, 1972) This is quite the opposite to our experience in Madras where urban evangelism became the key for planting churches in the villages.

The loss of members in the village congregation has been the gain of the city congregations, and we might add that on many occasions the loss of village members has been the gain of satan and his kingdom. These are the syndromes of the urbanized Christian community today. Discipling an urban population sometimes becomes more and more difficult, inspite of the opportunities for multiplying churches in urban India.

In Madras, again in sharp contrast to the Bombay experience, our city churches were not depending upon the Christian migrants - - though hundreds of unchurched, nominal Christians who otherwise could have been lost to the world were led to the

114

saving power of Christ. The most spectacular development of our churches during the last five years was the spread of churches to the villages.

It is high time that the churches and missions in India call their attention to the great need of discipling the responsive non-Christian populations in the ever-growing cities. There is nothing new in this. This was the strategy of St. Paul.

> By establishing the Church in two or three centers, St. Paul claimed that he had evangelized the whole province. Ten years after his first start from Antioch, he told the Romans that he had fully preached the Gospel of Christ from Jerusalem and round about Illyricum, and that he had no more place in these parts. In that single sentence we have the explanation and the justification of St. Paul's establishment of the churches in important centers in a province. When he had occupied two or three centeres, he had really and effectually occupied the province. (Allen 1930:19)

The missionary methods of Paul have been ours in Madras. While we worked to establish strong churches in the city, we never bypassed opportunities as they opened up to plant churches in rural areas. Such contacts mostly came through our own members of the city congregations, seminary students and pastors.

Men and women who came to the city seeking employment, happened to attend one of the churches, got saved, went back to their villages on holidays, shared with their relatives their new experiences, and build up a small group very friendly to Jesus Christ. Then they called us and we preached the Gospel, baptized believers and established new churches. An example of just this kind of church multiplication follows :

1. Kancheevaram Extension

Back in 1962, a man by the name of Mr. Thangaraj came to Madras from his small village called Ambi near Kancheevaram, which was about fifty miles southwest of Madras. He had a new job in the railway. Mr. Thangaraj came in contact with our church at Aminjikarai and through the influence of Rev. John G. Williams, the pastor, he and his family accepted Christ and were baptized.

Since then, Thangaraj has had a burden to bring his own Harijan relatives to Christ. Whenever he went back to his village fifty miles away, he told them about Christ and Christianity. As the people showed interest, Thangaraj told the pastor about it and this has resulted in both the pastor and Thangaraj making a trip to Ambi. Pastor John Williams was quite surprised at how the Lord had already begun His good work in the hearts of the people.

Rev. Williams frequently visited the village with Mr. Thangaraj and other lay people in the congregation. About twenty-five intimates of Mr. Thangaraj marvellously accepted Christ. No team of evangelists had been sent, no student camp had been held, but through strictly indigenous work of new Christians, twenty-five declared themselves ready to take baptism.

The pastors, seminary students, laymen, and the missionaries—hired a big bus one day in December, 1963, and went on a "pilgrimage" to take part in the great event at Ambi where twenty-two of the twenty-five were baptized in a nearby stream. It was a challenging and joyous occasion. It dawned on the church leaders that day that if twenty-two could be baptized with such "little" effort, there must be hundreds of other groups of ready listeners around the area who might be discipled for Christ.

Rev. John Williams volunteered to move from Madras to Kancheevaram to head the movement. Later on, two other graduates were appointed to help him. The movement did spread to three other villages. Meanwhile, Rev. John Williams resigned from the Mission as he could not accept the item policy of the Mission that wives should not work at secular jobs. Unfortunately, when he left the Mission, he took the Ambi congregation with him. Rev. G. A. Jeevavaram who succeeded him left the Mission on that ground also. It is our hope that we would have the privilege of having these able men back into our team at some stage.

116

These sudden changes of ledership did shake up the work. However, the present man who is in charge of the work, Rev. A. Amos reports :

> We have three organized churches in Kanchee-varam with seventeen members, in Panapakkam forty members, in Damal twenty members, with a total community of over two hundred people. A few high caste Hindus were led to the Lord through our book shop. One such young high caste Hindu young man who found Christ through the book store ministry is now studying in the Madras Bible Seminary, getting himself trained to become a minister. Our present need is a team of evangelists that we can use in evangelizing the many villages around. (Amos-Correspondence)

2. Jolarpet Extension

"Cast your bread upon the waters and after many days you will find it."

Jolarpet is a small town between Madras and Bangalore to the west ; ten miles from this town there is a small village called Vellanayakkaneri. From this village, God raised a young man through the ministry of the National Missionary Society. Aruldoss was a *peyoti*, a man who casts out demons. He and a relative. K. C. Jesudasan, in Jolarpet town, became Christians and joined the Madras Bible Seminary. During their training, they never forgot to pray for relatives back in the country. On their initiative, a summer camp was held in 1954 in their villages. I well remember how their people resisted the Gospel. However, the seed was faithfully sown. After their training in the seminary they were appointed as pastors in Madras. Rev. K. C. Jesudasan continued with the Mission, while Aruldoss left it to serve with the National Missionary Society.

Meanwhile, Mr. Gnanadoss, the son of Aruldoss' sister came to Madras to take a clerical job in the educational department of the state of Madras. Despite his Christian uncle, he was much opposed to Christianity. However, as he began to attend the church at CIT, he accepted Christ. Later he felt urged to become a full-time minister. So he resigned his post and joined the Madras Bible Seminary and became a full-time pastor. During these days one other young man from that area became a Christian and he also become a full-time minister. These four men never bypassed an opportunity to witness to their pcople. Gnanadoss took his Gospel Army of laymen with him many times and witnessed among his people. In 1972 twenty-five of his close relatives accepted Christ in a remarkable way and were baptized. Aruldoss, seeing the movement, left NMS to throw himiself into leading his people to Christ. At this stage he approached us to take the work. We first sent six evengelists to assist him. People as whole families decided to become Christians. They were all instructed from God's Word. July 7, 1972, was the date fixed for the great event in which eighty-one were baptized. A fewpassages I wrote in the Light of Life Magezine describe that great occasion :

> On July 7, 1972, our big, old van carrying a group of pastors of the Evangelical Christian Church of India was moving towards Jolarpet, a district 130 miles southwest of Madras. Several others of our pastors and evnngelists were coming by bus and train. As we traveled we sang with joy because today eighty-one of our recent converts were to be baptized.

> We gathered in the village of Vellanayak-kaneri, for it was here that there had been the largest response to the Gospel. The program began as scheduled. The converts, other young Christian believers, pastors and evangelists—about two hundred in all—assembled in front of Pastor Aruldoss' home. After commiting all to the Lord in prayer, we moved in procession toward the riverside, singing or "shouting" the old Tamil lyric,

'Men of God, the world is for Jesus – only, by love let us make it His own.' It was a historical procession ! It was a witness march.

As the procession reached the riverside the inquisitive Hindus started crowding round. After settling the people down near the baptismal site the converts were given spiritual edification and I went over the catechism with them : Then we all raised our hands and prayed to God to fill us with His Spirit. And the Lord answered our prayer. It was marvellous to hear all the young converts telling of the wonderful works of God.

Three ministers, including myself, got into the water and the candidates for baptism followed us, stepping in one after the other amidst singing and great rejoicing. All eighty-one were baptized in the name of the Father and of the Son and of the Holy Spirit. It was a very touching and thrilling moment when Rev. Gnanadoss baptized his own father who had been opposing him all these years.

On the following day we dedicated a new church, built by the converts from one of these villages.

Whatever name one may give to this movement, Mass Movement, Relatives' Movement— People's Movement, without a shadow of doubt, it is the movement of the Holy Spirit. In these last few days alone we have baptized altogether one hundred six new believers and the movement continues. (Light of Life, Oct., 1972)

Three churches have been organized. Aruldoss' brother donated land for a building in one village. Gnanadoss' relatives gave land to put up a hut church in another. Three buildings are now complete. Fifty other enquirers are now getting ready for baptism.

It is interesting to note that these churches have been planted within the radius of ten miles from the famous Christukula Ashram which has been functioning well over half a century in this area. The Ashram was established jointly by a national and a British foreigner, Dr. Savri Rayan Jesudason and Dr. Patton. Dr. Patton was a millionnaire who followed Dr. Jesudason and took his fortune with him from England. They bought about six hundred acres of land and built hospitals and did a splendid service among the community with the hope to reaeh the Hindus with the Gospel. It was from this area the Lord has been giving us these many precious souls.

Did the Ashram Programme prepare the hearts of the people around this area? I would like to think so. At the same time, if faithful fervent evangelism had been done along church growth lines, with the interest of planting churches, the Ashram ministry could have been much more productive. This is where the promoters of Ashram movement in India fail in their mission. If church planting ministry is not the ultimate aim of the Ashram method, these Ashrams will end up becoming just another more "Mission Compounds" however indigenous the Ashram movement might be.

3. From Madras to Cape Comerin

Our latest spontaneous extension in the ministry is the opening of few churches in the Cape Comerin area. These churches came into existence when Rev. P. J. Sadusingh visited his native place right after witnessing the mass baptism service at Jolarpet. The Lord stirred his heart to witness to his relatives in Cape Comerin. His friends and relatives quite enthusiastically rallied around him.

Since then, Rev. Sadhusingh felt led to move from Madras to cape comerin to head up the movement. Just within few months eleven churches have mushroomed in several parts of Kanya Kumari Nearly two hundred converts are getting ready for baptism. Requests are constantly pouring in from several groups of converts in this area to organize them into churches and to provide them with pastors.

The road from Madras to cape comerin is wide opened for the gospel. If we are going to grow at this rate we might reach our goal of 100 churches before 1980.

CHAPTER VIII—CONVERSION IN THE INDIAN SETTING

In India, "conversion" is a word around which controversy swirls. Consequently, it must be seen in the Indian setting. The Hindu believes that each man is born into a caste and literally cannot change his caste or changes it, which is highly offensive to Hindus. Furthermore, during the time of Moslem rule, it was common for segments of the population to be forcibly "converted to Islam—by making the entire multitude eat beef for example. Thus, "to convert" has highly objectionable overtones.

A.   WHAT IS CONVERSION ?

If one defines conversion either as forcibly adding people to one's community or as "requiring them to abandon their culture," it is easy to object to it. As most Hindus define it, conversion is truly reprehensible. However, Christian conversion is something entirely different than either of the procedures just described. There is nothing forcible about it and it does not mean cultural conversion.

Conversion is not proselyting in the sense of leading men to renounce their culture. It is not changing a label, so that former Hindus upon eating beef become Moslems. What is it then ? Dr. Stanley Jones says, "Conversion is a change in the character followed by an outer change of allegiance corresponding to that inner change.   (1969 : 16)

A Hindu told Dr. Jones one day that he would be baptized if Dr. Jones would give him twenty thousand rupees. Dr. Jones replied. "My brother, if you should lay down twenty thousand rupees at my feet and say, 'Please baptize me,' I would refuse it and you." (Ibid.) Then he goes on to say :

> Proselytism and conversion are poles apart, and
> to confuse them is to degrade the most precious
> thing that life holds—conversion. It is to
> confuse love and lust, beauty and ugliness, life
> and death. (Ibid.)

121

It is true. Strictly speaking, conversion is someone becoming a new person, or a "new child." As in Jesus' words, "Except ye be converted and become as little children, ye cannot enter the kingdom of heaven."

So then in a narrow sense, conversion is one's own personal encounter with God. It is a personal and individual matter. There has been much stress on this aspect of conversion for over fifty years in Christian churches and missions in India. Both national ministers and foreign missionaries have hesitated to baptize families and groups with so much criticism in the air, made by men like Mahatma Gandhi against "Christian proselytism." Perhaps partly as a result of this, the twentieth century saw the great Christian Ashram movement. In India, Ashrams placed emphasis on the deepening of the spiritual life of the Christian. Men and (sometimes) women were asked to come out and live in Ashrams for a few days or weeks. The Ashrams served as retreat centers for Christians, leading them to deeper Christian lives. There were few conversions of non-Christians through these Ashrams.

The word conversion is also used in a broad sense referring to people movements, and Christianizing of nations like the conversion of Rome, conversion of Europe, and conversion of England, and so on. In short, conversion applies to both individual and multi-individual decisions. I am referring to both aspects in my description of conversions in our ministry in Madras.

My emphasis is that only through conversion can a man become a member of a church. The inividual need not necessarily be one of our own direct converts, but he must have had a conversion experience at least some place else.

B. CLASSIFICATION OF CONVERSIONS

Having stated the possibility of two or more shades of meaning for the word conversion, I go on to classify the three different types of conversions which we observed in Madras. The diagram and the line graph in the next two pages speak for themselves the C^1 C^2 C^3 numerical growth during the last twenty years.

CONVERSIONS 1953—73

C¹ (Conversion I) — from non-Christian religious background.

C² (Conversion II) — from nominal Christian (Protestant or Catholic background)

C³ (Conversion III) — from Christian families in the ECI and biological growth i.e., children of our own families.

FIG. 6

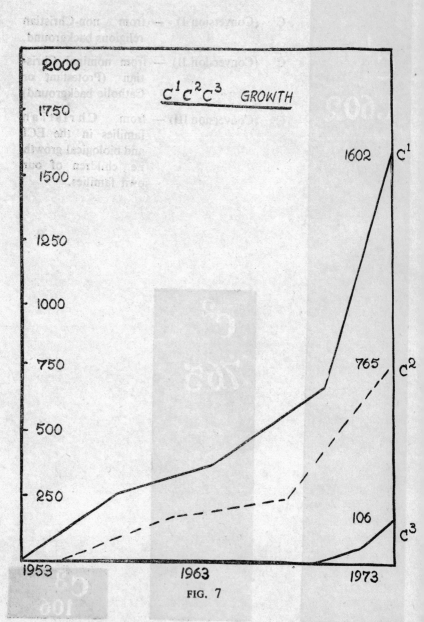

$C^1 C^2 C^3$ GROWTH

1602

765

1602

106

2000
1750
1500
1250
1000
750
500
250

1953
1963
1973

C^1
C^2
C^3

FIG. 7

My purpose is to give here "ways into a church." This is usually classified as conversions from non-Christian religions, transfers, and biological growth. Using these symbols (C¹, C², C³) the growth of a local church as well as the churches in a district may be classified.

C. Some Instances of Conversions

Both in the city and in the villages, where God led us, people found Christ in remarkable ways. In the case of some, they had already come under the influence of the Gospel through some one else.

1. An Alcoholic

At the age of five, Perumal was brought from a village about fifty miles from Madras by his *chinnamma* (aunt) because his mother had died and there was no one to take care of him. All this happened some twenty years ago. Perumal went to school until he was eleven years old. After this, his *chinnamma* sent him along with someone to Mysore State to work as a *cooli* (laborer) in the tea estates. At the age of eleven, Perumal learned to support himself. He worked hard and earned money, but fell in with bad company.

Those were days when there was strict prohibition against alcoholic beverages. Perumal joined a "company" which was illegally manufacturing *arrack*, a cheap and harmful drink, and learned how to make and smuggle it from place to place. He also became addicted to it. He was arrested by the police several times, beaten up, and put in jail.

Having gone to the extremity of his sinful life, Perumal came to the end of his resources and began to think of home. Meanwhile, his *chinnamma* back in Kilpauk, Madras had found a new religion and new hope in Jesus Christ. She renounced all her idols and became a Christian. As a widow, she was free to make this decision for herself, and for her children and became a member of the Kilpauk Church. Perumal lost all his money and friends and decided to quit Mysore State before he got into more trouble.

Like the prodigal son, he started his journey back to Madras and traveled five hundred miles without a ticket. His *chinnamma* was quite surprised to see him back. She was reluctant to receive him since she thought she was going to have an added burden in her family. However, she soon found a job for him and tried to get him settled in life. But Perumal continued to drink and could not give up his bad habits. He never attended church with his *chinnamma*.

In 1967, we had a week of gospel meetings in the church. One night his *chinnamma* and cousins did not get back home from the meeting so Perumal went to the church to escort them home. As he arrived at the church, the people were singing the last hymn. He was struck by the atmosphere of the meeting and resolved to attend the following nights. During those days, Perumal accepted Christ in a miraculous way. The Lord wonderfully delivered him from all his evil habits. He has been married since then and is an active youth leader in the church.

2. A Murderer

Veeramuth was his name. It meant "the pearl of bravery." The name was given to him by the villagers because of his brave deeds. In his early days he moved with his family from a suburban village to Arumbakkam of Madras.

Since he had no job, he got into the business of selling illicit alcohol. He became a terrible drunkard. He was also secretly in love with a woman other than his wife. On account of this, there were big quarrels between him and another group. In a brawl, one of the other party was killed and Veeramuth was sentenced to several years of imprisonment.

While in prison someone gave him a tract about Jesus Christ. His thoughts went back to what he had heard from Christians in the village. He had also seen Christians kneeling in prayer. So,

Veeramuth knelt down in prayer before God and muttered some prayers. He found a great peace in his own heart. He became a changed person. The prison authorities by seeing his changed life recommended that he be released from prison.

Returning home, he went to see the pastor of the local ECI congregation and dedicated his life to Christ. He and his entire family became Christians. He changed his name to "Vethamuthu" —the pearl of Scripture. He is now persuading his relatives to follow Christ. His testimony is a great challenge to the people of his village.

3. " Met God in Prison "

We have in our ranks students who were led to Christ through our ministry, who later on responded to God's call for full-time ministry. Some young men were led by others but were persuaded by us to join our team. Manoharan was one day going down the main street of Kancheevaram and read a scripture text in one of our book stores, "Jesus Christ came to the world to save sinners." He got down from his cycle and went into the book store, inquired from our pastor about the meaning of the text. In weeks, this young man was led to Christ.

Jonie Raj Sekar as a young boy of sixteen joined a militant communist group. One day two men from the secret police department were following him on suspicion. Sekar slipped into a church to bewilder the policemen. It was a Friday evening. The people in the church were having a prayer meeting. Sekar gave his heart to Christ that night. He is now a student in the seminary getting himself trained to be an evangelist.

The story of K. Devadoss is still more remarkable. Devadoss had been the village postman and had a passion for gambling. This led him to forge a money order one day so that he could pursue his passion further. But he was caught in the city of Madras, where he had fled, some three hundred fifty miles from his village, and was taken back to be imprisoned in Madurai.

127

During his time in the Madurai Central Jail, a Christian evangelist came to conduct services for the prisoners. But Devadoss mocked him, loudly extolling virtues of the Hindu gods, and doing his best to prevent others from hearing the message. His insolence, however, could not remedy the horrible loneliness and shame that he felt inside.

One day when he was scarcely able to contain his despair, Devadoss looked up to see the evangelist at the door of his cell. Opening his heart, Devadoss told him about his crime and of the hopelessness he felt.

The evangelist counseled Devadoss, and gave him a tract which told of an older brother who willingly assumed the role of his younger brother and went to the murderer's gallows in his place. This illustration of Christ's great sacrificial love touched Devadoss deeply. He read and reread the tract some forty times.

On New Year's Eve, 1967, Devadoss opened his heart to Jesus. He gives his testimony :

> I began repenting of my sins and invited Jesus
> to come into my heart. When I accepted Him
> as my own personal Saviour, it was a night of
> rejoicing. All my burdens and sins of my heart
> rolled away. " (Rabe, "Standard " Feb., 1973)

A changed attitude and life soon caught the attention of the warden, and Devadoss was discharged from prison before his nine-month sentence expired. He is now a senior in Madras Bible Seminary.

4. "Money Could Not Buy Peace and Healing"

What tremendous growth a church can experience when a family of twelve decide for Christ and join the church. In 1968, Esther Amma and her husband and their ten children did away with the numerous Hindu gods they worshipped, took baptism, and became members of our church at Villiwakkam.

128

Esther Amma, before she became a Christian, was married to a rich young man when she was only fourteen years old. By the age of nineteen she had had four children, developed fits, and was hospitalized for well over three months. Esther's husband was running a very flourishing business in Madras, so they spent their fortune consulting one doctor after another, finding no improvement.

Then some of her husband's friends and businessmen told them that if they offered their hair to Lord Venkateswara (a famous deity in South India reputed to have power to heal people and make them rich) she might find healing.

> Year after year [says Esther] we went to Venkateswara Temple as a whole family. We got our heads shaved and offered our hair. We went on doing like this eight times until I was twenty-seven years old. Meanwhile, my husband incurred a big loss in the business. Having become no better in my mind with all the disappointments in life, I decided to commit suicide by taking poison. The poison, however, did not harm me. Strange are the ways of God that He had a concern for me and for my family long before I accepted Him. (Tract 5:2)

As the family did not have the money to go to Venkateswara Temple for the ninth time, they shaved their hair in their own home and kept it to be offered at the temple at some later date. Just at this time, by divine providence, Esther Amma met an old Christian friend who explained to her the way of salvation and how Christ could heal her. For about three months Esther Amma secretly attended Christian meetings. God miraculously healed her. Her husband, hearing of her interest in Christianity, began to persecute her, but as he heard more of the Gospel, he yielded to truth and took baptism. Both husband and wife with their ten children became members of our church at Villivakkam. And once again their business prospered.

129

5. A Hindu Priest

Senthamangalam Pudoor is a village about ten miles from Kancheevaram and sixty miles south of Madras. In Chapter VII I have described how the opening came for us to extend our ministry to Kancheevaram.

Rev. M. Moni was our pioneer minister there. One evening in 1966, as he was going around distributing tracts he came to a place where he saw a group of people standing before a small Hindu shrine. The priest was inside doing *pooja* (chanting prayers). The people outside were waiting for him to come out and "bless" them. He did come out in a few minutes under demon possession and told fortunes to the people gathered there. Before the people dispersed, Pastor Moni distributed tracts to them. The priest objected to this. But from time to time, Pastor Moni went to that temple to distribute the tracts.

One day after much prayer, Mr. Moni went to the priest's home and gave him a tract. The priest read it and began to take an interest in the Christian religion. Mr. Moni kept meeting him for several weeks. He gave him biographies of Sadhu Sundar Singh and Narayan Vaman Thilak to read.

God began to work in the heart of the priest. One day he went to brother Moni's house to see him. On that day and on the days following, Mr. Moni explained to the priest the way of salvation. The priest miraculously accepted Christ. This made a big stir in the village as the priest refused to do *pooja* in the temple.

Eight of his relatives gave their hearts to Christ and were baptized. The priest took a new name—Abel. For many years he shared his testimony in many churches and in public meetings. He has now gone to be with the Lord, but his testimony still lives on in the village.

6. Deliverance from Demon Possession and Witchcraft

Many in both cities and villages in India are under the influence of demons in one form or another. Hundreds and thousands of such people are delivered from possession when Spirit-filled Christians pray for them. This is an important Christian ministry in India.

Almost all of our pastors are called in to pray for the sick and cast out demons. God has given two of our men special gifts. They fill their churches with people who are weaned away from demonism. On a few occasions, Christians who fail to walk close with God still succumb to the evil spirits. Two of the latest case histories of deliverance from demon possession are worthy of mention.

a. " *Mohini* "—The Demon of Sexual Love

Chandran, a young man, a nephew of a famous cinema star in South India by the name of Mathuruthevi, was working with a shipping company. He used to be found at home only three months during the year. The rest of the year he was on his tours from country to country. During his three-month holiday in 1972, he came to live with his uncle in Red Hills where Rev. P. M. Daniel is the pastor of the ECI Church.

Chandran came to know about Mr. Daniel who is gifted with healing. He attended the ECI one Sunday and asked the pastor to pray for him. For well over seven years, Chandran was suffering from a dreadful disease. During a day he would have at least three times at uncontrollable discharge and fall into convulsions. He had consulted able doctors on his tours and had taken all kinds of medicine to no avail.

One Friday night brother Daniel went to pray for him. As he laid his hands on him in prayer, Chandran began to dance and came under evil possession and taking a clearly feminine voice said, "Do you know who I am? I am Nalini. I studied in St. Mary's College. I love Chandran. I have been with him for the last seven years serving him as a humble wife. I love Chandran."

Mr. Daniel immediately discerned in his spirit that this demon was a *Mohini* (an enchantress). He prayed over Chandran. After a long struggle, Nalini left Chandran's body. Then Chandran told his story to brother Daniel.

Sir, when I was studying in my college, I loved a girl by the name of Nalini. We both were inseparable and loved each other so much. She

131

had been suffering from some unbearable pain in her stomach that no doctors could heal. Nalini thought she was going to die soon and that when she would die she would die at my feet. Weeks later as Nalini could not stand her stomach pain any longer she took poison to commit suicide and was admitted in the hospital. When I went to see her at the hospital. she rose from her bed and fell down at my feet and died. Since that time onward, I was under the grip of some kind of fear. I felt that a woman was with me all the time. When I went to bed she would go to bed with me. Though for some time I enjoyed her constant presence with me, I could not stand the ordeal of the same kind of ailment which took away Nalini's life. In this way I spent nearly seven years of my life. But now I feel a great relief in my body. (Daniel, Letter correspondence)

saying this, Chandran really jumped with great joy for what the Lord had done for him. He took baptism on January, 1973. He is witnessing to his Hindu relatives about the Lord.

b. *Glossalalia*—a Case of Speaking in Tongues Through Evil Spirit

Shantha and her family were active members of the church. For about four years she suffered from an unsual disease that no doctors could cure. She finally went to a *Peyotti* (witch doctor). The *Peyotti* instead of relieving her of the ailment, attempted to rape her. When Shantha refused to yield to him, he sent an evil spirit into her. From that time onward she became a very miserable person.

After some months she attended a Pentecostal meeting expecting deliverance from the trouble she had. There she began speaking in tongues. Shantha and other Pentecostals thought she was filled with the Holy Spirit. But in reality it was the demon in her that made her to act that way as she found no release from her troubles. Though there was no change in her life, she would always dress herself in white and attend Pentecostal meetings, speaking in tongues day in and day out. But mentally, physically and spiritually she was suffering because of the possession of this demon.

At this time she and her husband came to live in Red Hills and came in contact with Rev. P. M. Daniel and his church. One Friday evening during the prayer meeting Shantha was filled with the "spirit" and shouted "Shipratheep, Sheenkar, Sheekara, Sheekma, Sheekra, Thuse, Shante Theba, Sheepra, Shinkari, Sheekma, Sheekma Thuse, Shenkara."

Mr. Daniel immediately caught hold of the hair of the lady and asked her to give the interpretation of the tongues. Thereupon she replied, "The interpretation is : Oh, head-mistress of the demons give your power. Oh, headman of the demons give me your power." The demon threatened to kill brother Daniel, but after a great struggle it swore and left Shantha. Now she is completely free from the trouble she had. Her husband is a deacon in the church.

D. Sociological Factors in Conversions

1. Problems Faced by Converts Who Come as Individuals

The western man looks at religion from a different perspective than the people of the so-called underdeveloped countries. The urbanized westerner thinks of man's relation with God as primarily an individual and personal matter. The Indian considers religion as a group concern. Dr. McGavran suggests several causes for this. One is the social structure of the West in which there are few exclusive subsocieties. However, many of these exist in many parts of the eastern world. In the West, unlike in India, "one member of a family can become a Christian and live as a Christian without being ostracized by the rest of the family." (McGavran 1955 : 8)

Conversion of individuals often do not last long. Family pressures are very strong on individuals who accept Christ. We have lost some high caste converts because of their dependance on

133

their families. One Brahmin young man changed his old name Gopal to Paul Milton, and was used mightily of the Lord. Many were blessed through his testimony. He joined our seminary and seemed to be doing well, but in the third year of his training, he left the school and went back into "the world." The pressures from his family were too strong for him to bear.

2. Place of Urbanization in Conversion

The family system—to a degree at least—breaks down when members of a family migrate to the city. As they move to the city they are naturally free from their family unit though they maintain roots in their families back in the villages. New settlers to the city are mostly open to anything. They constantly look for fellowship and the community life which the village has been providing for them. Great opportunity exists to multiply churches among immigrants.

Forty-one of the fifty converts interviewed told us that they accepted Christ after coming to the city. Most of them had already heard about Christ in their native places but felt unable to decide for Christ in the midst of their relatives. In Kaveripakkam, a young Muslem, Mohmad Ali, a teacher in a high school, gave his heart to Christ. He could not have done this had he been back in his native place.

3. How and When Web Movements Occur

By web movements, I mean multi-individual decisions for Christ involving small units (one or two nuclear families) at a time, but all of one homogeneous unit.

People who become members of a church as groups and families stand together as a unit. They always make better Christians than those who are picked as individuals from here and there and brought together into a conglomerate church. Where acceptance of Christianity has been "communal," the decisions are often made by small units or subgroups within the people. Seldom are they made by the people as a whole. It must be recognized :

Those churches arising out of group movements do not consist of aggregates of individuals

134

brought together by random or by mutual interest in the Christian religion. They were a sociological unit before they became Christians. (Brandenfels 1963 : 6)

Web movements usually begin with one or two individuals. If such individuals are soundly born again and on fire for the Lord in a matter of a few years all of their families are brought into the Christian fold. If the conversion of the first individuals was not solid, or was wrongly motivated, it might stop with such individuals. In other cases, it might result in their isolation or moving back into the old society and old ways.

Sometimes web movements occur spontaneously. An immediate recognition of a web movement and quick attention to it can help the movement spread rapidly. This is exactly what is happening in the ECI ministries spreading out from the city to villages. People movements and web movements also occur as a result of well thought-out strategies and hard, bold plans.

However, in a deeper sense, the Holy Spirit is the real cause of all conversions — of individuals and of groups. He uses the social structure and we, seeking to be sensitive to His leading, work at His direction to build Christ's Church.

Church Planting in Action

Street Preaching

REV. P. M. DANIEL, one of
our several men who are gifted
with healing and casting out
demons.

136

Our Beloved Missionaries
THE HOUGHTONS

Few of the First Converts Baptized at Saidapet River in 1955

There's always a great Rejoicing at Baptism

Rev. GNANADOSS baptizing his own father who has been opposing him all these years

Mass Baptism at Jolarpet

One of the many Churches mushrooming
all over Kanyakumari District

Multiplying Churches means not necessarily
multiplying "Buildings" But our
congregation at Saidapet
decided to put up this
beautiful place of worship

CHAPTER IX — SOME MISSIOLOGICAL FACTORS IN CHURCH GROWTH

I shall, in this chapter, summarize some of the missiological factors and causes for the growth of the Evangelical Church of India in the city of Madras and in Tamilnadu during the last twenty years.

A. ENVIRONMENTAL FACTORS

1. The Culture of the Tamilians

As I have already mentioned in the first chapter, the culture of the South Indians was in many ways quite different from that of the North Indians. Much of our knowledge of the original Dravidian culture has been gained from the study of the Dravidian words still used in Tamil. Especially we find a series of remarkable words which denote and describe sin. These show that the Dravidians possessed a clearness of moral vision no less remarkable than that of the ancient Hebrews. (Sargent, 1960 : 3) There is some truth in this assumption and the Tamilians appear to have a capacity for the Gospel. Christianity has been more at home in the South than in the North.

2. Political Factors — The Anti-Brahmin Movements

The next important environmental factor in the growth of the church is a political one. Hinduism in India is Brahminism. During the last half of this century, Tamilnadu fathered an anti-Brahmin and anti-Hindu movement which I have described in the first chapter. Out of this movement, a strong political party, the DMK, emerged and became the ruling party of the state since 1967. The movement was very popular among the masses. It is an exaggeration to say that the DMK has done away with religion in South India; but, undoubtedly, it has weaned the suppressed masses from the clutches of Brahminism, and to a certain extent, has created a religious vacuum among them. Perhaps this is one of the causes for the small people movements and church growth the OMS-ECI has experienced.

3. Secular and Urban Mood

Secularism may look like a dangerous trend in Europe and other countries. Though one might not fully agree with Harvey Cox's "secular theology" which celebrates the process of secularization of the world as the logical outcome of biblical religion, there is some truth in his argument that:

> Secularization implies a historical process, almost certainly irreversible, in which society and culture are delivered from tutelage to religious control and closed metaphysical world views . . . it is basically a liberating development. (1967 : 18)

This liberating development is taking place right now in India where centuries - old religious domination is breaking up in some circles. The urban outlook is to be felt not only in the towns and cities but even in the remote rural areas. When I was doing my pioneer ministry in Porur, the villagers used to tell me, "we no longer fear ghosts and devils in the night because our village is now electrified with luminous lights; the ghosts have moved to the jungles."

I am not affirming that people are free from the fear of evil spirits and are no longer slaves to superstitions. My observation here is simply this : India is today in the grip of urbanism and urbanization. The change is taking place not only in the cities but an urban mood prevails even in the villages. In other words the mood for change has come and I consider this a great opportunity. Wherever we sensed God's direction and leading, we immediately moved in. A tremendous amount of church growth followed.

142

My conclusion is that what we have experienced and found to be somewhat successful in Madras could be applied on a much larger scale and churches planted among any responsive community in an urban area.

4. Christian Heritage in Tamilnadu

Christianity took root in Tamilnadu possibly as early as the first century and certainly by 1600. Though there has been no visible form of a Tamil Church from the first century, it is a well accepted conjecture that the message of Jesus Christ reached Kerala during the first four centuries.

For the last four hundred years, both Roman Catholic and Protestant missionaries came to the South and established churches of their respective denominations. The Tamilians always speak highly of the Christian missionary's contribution to the Tamil literature. The selfless service of the missionaries in the fields of education and their humanitarian enterprises are generally praised by the people of Tamilnadu. Besides this kind of influence, the Christian presence is very much felt by virtue of the fact that 5·7 per cent of the population in the state and 6·2 per cent in the city of Madras are Christian. It is an obvious fact that Madras is the largest Christian city in India.

Though the existing Protestant denominations could not care about evangelizing the millions of Tamilnadu, the impact of Christian religion is a historical reality in the Southland.

5. The After effects of the 1905 Revival in Madras

Dr. J. Edwin Orr writes :

> Many in Madras were praying for an out-
> pouring of the Holy Spirit in all of Tamilnadu
> in 1905. The Madras Missionary Conference
> had issued a call to prayer and was already
> reporting that revival had begun. (1970:88)

In my third chapter I mentioned how out of this revival the Madras Bible League was born at Zion Church. The OMS missionaries, who themselves were products of revival in the

West, were greatly welcomed by the Bible League in 1951 and 1955 before OMS entered Madras. Rev. D. Samuel, Rev. E. Victor Joseph, the early co-founders of OMS ministry in India, were men who came from these awakenings. They were also laboring together with Bakht Singh for many years before they joined OMS.

Rev. P. Devabuktie, the editor of the OMS Tamil Revival Magazine, and a teacher in the seminary for some time, came from the revival movements in Dohnavur Fellowship which Dr. Orr talks about. Mr. Devabuktie persuaded me to apply to the Madras Bible Seminary. I myself, as a boy, had been in a revival movement back in the Tirunelveli District. My father came to know the Lord through one of the converts of the famous CMS missionary, Rev. T. Walker of Tirunelveli during whose time there were great awakenings in South India. My father was a well known revivalist and a great man of prayer. He has influenced my life tremendously.

So, in many ways, quite a number of us in the OMS can be said to have come out of the revival in Tamilnadu. The aftereffect of the revival is felt even today in Madras. The groups of believers who are the offshoots of the revival, like Madras Bible League and The Pilgrim Progress Team, who are known for their passion for souls, did from time to time help in our church planting ministry. Revival in a small measure has occurred in the midst of our pastors and congregations very often. Summarizing the relation of revival to church growth, Dr. McGavran says :

> Revival is like a head of steam in a railway engine. Without it the engine remains motionless. With it, plus rails, pistons, water, oil, timetables, engineer, and other elements, the engine travels widely and fast. Great growth of the church following revival will come when all the conditions are right. So right, in fact, that people are not conscious of them. This was the case of Pentecost which is the prime example of the bearing of revival on church growth. (1970:180)

B. ROLE OF THE FOREIGN MISSION - OMS

1. The Structure

There is a Tamil proverb which says, "You can never paint a picture without a wall to paint on." It is hard to function effectively without, as it were, some kind of a structure to lean on. In the OMS, which is devoted fully to the cause of establishing churches, we found such a structure.

2. Clear Objectives and Policies

It is the definite policy of the OMS International in Madras to promote revival among churches and to call Indian men and women to train Tamilian Christians to serve among their own people. To quote the objectives of the Mission :

> From the beginning, it has been an undenomi-
> national society with a threefold emphasis
> upon (a) the establishing of Bible seminaries
> and institutions (b) intensive and extensive
> evangelism, and (c) the establishment of
> indigenous, self-governing, self-supporting and
> self-propagating national churches in various
> countries in which it operates. (E.C.I. Manual,
> 1972)

These being the basic objectives and policies of the Mission, our objectives are very clear and we are on a sure foundation.

3. Mission's Previous Experience in Church Planting

The founder's vision to train national leaders and to evangelize the nations through the nationals was by and large fulfilled in the other countries of the Orient where the Mission had served earlier. Churches were planted by the hundreds in Korea, Japan, and China. The OMS has always been a church-planting mission. This remarkable experience the Mission had in the past with the battles fought and the victories won has contributed enormously to the overall strategy of the Mission.

Many early OMS missionaries to India had undergone persecution in China. They also witnessed the plight of the national churches under Communist takeover. Through this kind of experience, the Mission knew what it meant to suffer for the sake of the Gospel. The Mission withstood all these fiery tests and emerged stronger than ever.

With years of experience in the Orient, the Society became skillful in making the right decisions and handling affairs properly.

4. The Mission Subsidy

It is a well known fact that most of the denominations, including some which are over two hundred years old still receive some kind of foreign aid. Even churches like the CSI and the CNI, which are under full "self-support," receive considerable assistance toward church activities such as community service, orphanages, and hospitals.

In India as well as in all the countries which were under colonial rule, the financial pattern in churches and mission has been one of "investment" in which the sending mission body financed the mission field activities and sub-sidized the budget for the established churches until they became able to support their own positions. This pattern will continue for some time for even the current philosophy of indigenity and self-support is something which has been advocated by the foreign missions but which has yet to be accepted by the national churches.

The ministry of OMS International in Madras and in other parts of India could not have begun and three thousand souls could not have been discipled had not the Society sent its missionaries to break the ground and to lay the foundation. This, the Evangelical Church of India, fully appreciates.

The OMS aids the National Church not only to plant churches but to nurture them for a certain period until they come to self-support. In 1973. the congregations raised $ 500 per month toward the salary of the pastors and the OMS contributed $ 1,000. This salary is distributed to twenty-seven national workers. Within five years we hope to bring all the Madras churches under self-support. But until then, Mission subsidy is necessary. Mission aid is also necessary to plant the seventy new churches planned for the decade and for the continuous functioning of the seminary which feeds trained pastors into the field.

5. Men For Missions International (MFMI)

Besides the steady flow of financial support for the workers. there is yet another American service known as MFMI through which the Lord provides fund for church planting in Madras City.

MFMI, a layman's wing of OMS was born as a result of a spontaneous movement among American Christians associated with the OMS. In this organisation, thousands of men of multiple church affiliations and every walk of life have found a channel for harnessing and releasing personal skills and abilities in practical, direct missionary participation in overseas witness-and-work crusades. They have been fired with new zeal for soul winning at home as well as abroad. (Pearsons 1967: 124).

In 1969–1970, MFMI took India as its projects and made available nearly $ 15,000. With these God-sent funds, we were able to buy land for churches in the city so that permanent buildings for worship could be erected.

Several house churches which came dangerously close to being closed got on their feet and grew tremendously when church building sites were purchased for them from the MFMI funds.

Our church at Basin Bridge, North Madras, was established as early as 1955, but had no permanent place of worship. Until 1964, the meetings were conducted in a hut on rented land. The owner notified the congregation to vacate the property. The bewildered congregation went and approached the nearby YMCA to allow its small building for two hours of worship on Sunday mornings. After two years even this place was no longer available. There was no other suitable hall where worship could be continued, as the houses of the believers were too small to have any kind of meeting. The only possibility was to attach the congregation to a nearby church at Otteri. The disappointed congregation found it hard to go to another church. A few faithful did attend, but others scattered.

After an unhappy year in 1968, the MFMI gave a substantial amount of $ 2,000 for the purchase of land and building. This immediately took care of the problem. Services were resumed. The scattered members began coming back. New members were added to the church, and there was a rapid growth. Within one year, the membership grew forty to one hundred and twenty. The church in 1972 still continues to grow.

The point that I am emphasizing here is obvious. This church could not have gotten on its feet but for the timely help from the Society through MFMI.

It is my conviction that for an effective, speedy church planting ministry in India, the Evangelical Church in India is going to have to rely on foreign funds until we get many churches of our own which can build up funds for church extension. Even after evolving a healthy indigenous means by which we might disciple people, the present system must continue as the opportunities in India are enormous. Some Christians have pledged themselves not to receive foreign funds for the evangelization of India. While we understand their earnestness, we must ask how much evangelization such men are actually doing ? How many churches have they started ? Let us not get carried away by flaming enthusiasm and say to ourselves, " One soul brought to salvation by Indian rupees is worth one hundred souls brought in by American dollars." However, we do have to bear in mind that an ideal missionary method would be the kind of fully self-supporting one which St. Paul practiced and we do have to require every church in India to dedicate perhaps a tenth of its giving to planting other churches.

An unevangelizing stagnant Indian Church has beeen sitting in one corner of India for the last two thousand years and unless it reforms itself, it will sit there for another two thousand years

Seated in the same gallery are the united churches of North and South India. Churches which are not evangelizing are not really churches. There is no life in them. They are dead. They are like the dry bones and fossils which tell us of antiquity. But these lazy churches have the "courage" to criticize evangelizing agencies which (maybe with a little foreign aid) are in the field planting churches. This kind of mentality must go. Churches must give priority to church planting. No matter who does it, how they do it, and by what resources they do it, this has got to be done.

C. LEADERSHIP ROLE.

I mentioned earlier Rev. E. L. Kilbourne's concern to get "the right type of men" to evangelize the cities. One of the great causes for church growth is that God sent or raised among us such "right type" of leaders.

1. Missionary Leadership.

Under whatever handicaps the missionaries might have had to operate, their words and decisions have carried much weight. Dynamic national leadership in the post colonial era, has not emerged even in large denominations like CSI which have found no way of reproducing the missionary passion once the western bishop left. Though the Britishers are out of India, "the British" is not out of the Indians yet ! The words of the *Saheb* (the Hindi word for the white man) are always "divinely inspired words." Whether they took right or wrong decisions, their decisions were always final.

On the whole, missionary leadership in the absence of national leadership has been one of the chief causes of church growth.

Rev. G. Garnett Phillippe, one of the co-founders of the ministry in Madras was a man who suffered for Christ in China and knew what it means to count the cost for the sake of the Gospel. Dr. David J. Rigby gave up his medical practice to become a missionary. The experience he gained in British Guiana,

149

his ability to grasp things quickly and understand situations and his foresight, have greatly contributed toward laying a foundation for church planting. It was through insights that he had gained from experience and acquired through books and personal interviews with senior missionaries in India that the OMS launched in out into a full scale church planting ministry.

Rev. Rudolf M. Rabe, who succeeded Dr. Rigby from 1960 to 1963, consolidated the work and bought the property for the seminary, which we were renting until 1960.

Hiring workers is easy in India, but not firing them ! Down through the years the OMS accumulated some unworthy leaders. It was Rev. J. Ferris who took a bold step in removing these, purifying the work.

Rev. Joe Black took charge from 1970 to 1972—a very critical time in which church administration was being handed over to the nationals. The Manual of ECI was also enforced in the churehes where the by-laws had not been fully applied.

The philosophy of missionary leadership after the handing over of the responsibilities has been considerably changed. Rev Graham Houghton, a brilliant, young missionary (who is now the Mission Representative to the National Church, and the Principal of the Bible Seminary) feels that a missionary can still play the role of an innovator.

2. National Leadership

An unusual blending of talents and personalities is found in our team, perhaps more than in any other mission assisted church in India. God has brought together men of various backgrounds and capacities but sharing a common vision.

Every one of the twenty-six pastors and evangelists except one or two were trained in our seminary and know our program very well. Every pastor is a born again child of God. All have had remarkable conversions.

Nearly half of the twenty-six men are converts from Hinduism whom we led to the Lord during the early days of our ministry. This makes them loyal to the ECI and emotionally involved with our program.

Every one of them has a powerful testimony. The present pastor of Arumbakkam, Rev. N. J. Gnanaraj, as a young man during his college years became so disappointed in life that he took poison to kill himself. His attempt failed and later he accepted Christ and applied to the seminary. Rev. P. J. Sadhu-singh spent his life in bars roaming from place to place before he miraculously found the Lord. Rev. S. Aruldoss was a *peyotti* (witchdoctor). His sister's son, Rev. Gnanadoss was militant against Christianity. Sundararajan was an active Communist leader. Rev. Devadoss, as a government postman forged the signature on a money order and took the money for gambling. He landed in Jail for it and the Lord met him there. These and other men who have tasted of the love of Christ are in a position to guide men to the Lord in a more realistic way. Their spiritual leadership in the churches is perhaps the main factor that has contributed to the growth of ECI.

The graph on the following page shows how rapidly the church has been growing ever since the administration of the churches was handed over to the nationals from 1969.

D. STRATEGIES AND METHODS

So much vague and foggy thinking is found among those who are supposed to be involved in a church planting ministry "In missions" says Dr. McGavran, "it is common to assume that church growth will take place without planning." (1970:354). There are those who think that "human planning" is not of the Holy Spirit. But we have to bear in mind that our God is a God who *acts,* but He usually works through human channels. God seldom seems to work through men who have no vision or a sense of goal. "Where there is no vision, people perish."

1. Concentrating on the Responsive Segments.

Sowing must be done on good soil with a concentrated effort. "Today's paramount task, opportunity, and imperative in missions, is to multiply churches in the increasing numbers of respective peoples of the earth." (McGavaran 1970 : 63),

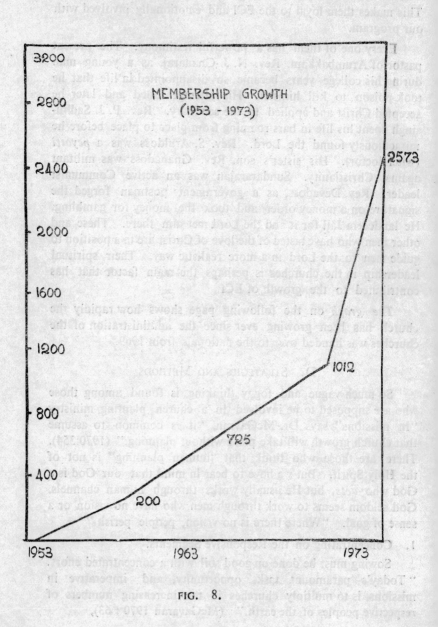

MEMBERSHIP GROWTH
(1953 - 1973)

3200

2800

2573

2400

2000

1600

1200

1012

800

725

400

200

1953   1963   1973

FIG. 8.

Whether in the city or in the suburbs, the ECI and the OMS in Madras were preaching to all castes with a special ministry to Harijans. In the earlier year we concentrated on high caste communities, like the Brahmins with very slight or even no results. One or two young men accepted Christ but soon went back to "the world". In the later years, God led us to pay particular attention to the Harijans and our success has always been among the so-called low caste people. The natural tendency often has been to publicize conversions from the so-called " high caste " people and say less about conversions from the "low caste" commuity, but we now recognize this tendency as a mistake.

I must confess that we have not concentrated on this supplessed mass of people enough to have the kind of people movements we desire. Missionaries have often advised us not to go to the low caste. In a settlement or a village of all castes, the strategy has been, to try and find a "nutral" place where people of all castes could assemble. This policy has not been successful. But wherever we were forced to confine our efforts to one ethnic group, there has been tremendous church growth. It has taken God several years to prove to us that He wanted us to concentrate on the responsive masses. Erukkamanagar, Arumbakkam, Otteri, Saidapet, Madhuravoil. Ayyapakkam, Trustpuram, Porur, Thirupathur, and Nattramballi Churches are overwhelmingly monoethnic churches. These churches stand together better than the conglomerate churches. They grow much more rapidly than the multiethnic congregations.

2. Preach, Persuade, Plant.

The communists have their local strategies and world strategies. Political parties have their techniques to win an election. What is Christian strategy in the mission field?

Our strategy in Madras is to preach the Gospel—to persuade the people—and to plant churches. These precepts are scriptural and are enshrined in Christ's great commission. Our Lord has commanded us to go to all, preach to all, baptize all and teach all *jatis* (ethnics and peoples).

153

OUR THREE FOLD STRATEGY :
PREACH — PERSUADE — PLANT

FIG. 9

We need today a ministry of persuasion, a ministry of discipling. With this specific strategy, we in the OMS and the ECI spend our time, energy, talent and money in a very systematic, organized way. A tremendous amount of preaching is going on today but in many cases much of the sowing is done on the wayside and upon rocks and among the thorns and the thistles. All churches should renounce such poor strategy.

3. Power Encounter. ——

The world today is looking for a sign. The moment people see the power of God demonstrated, He begins to work in their hearts. Our Lord said, "Behold I give you power (*exousia*)...... over all the power (*dunamis*)". Lk. 10 : 19.

Dr. Tippet says that in the eye of any potential Melanesian convert to Christanity, the issues was one of power in daily life. The convert could not stand with the missionary or evangelist and conceptualize in terms of psychology and western thought forms. Rather, the missionary had to stand with the convert and help him to understand what Christ meant in terms of power encounter. (1967 : 5).

In a non-Christian community like India, the power encounter is very effective. Quite a number of our pastors are men gifted with healing and casting out of demons. When God brings healing to one member of the Hindu family, it influences the rest of the family and relatives,

Notable among these "divine healers" is Rev. P. M. Daniel, now pastor of the church at Red Hills. When he was appointed in this unevangelized area in 1967, Daniel started the church with one Christian family. As a result of power encounter in that suburban village, the church has been growing very rapidly. The baptized membership of that church today has gone upto sixty-five. Nearly two-thirds of the congregation are people who became Christians because healing came to their bodies through prayer and the laying on of hands or they were delivered from demon possession.

4. Releasing the Lay Potentiality.

Any pastor who mobilizes the entire congregation will find the church filling up. People like to feel that they are "somebody". This is human nature. Any leader who recognizes the many talents in his congregation, and without feeling jealous about it, encourages each Christian to express and demonstrate his talents, finds that he is releasing a great surge of power. He calls people to action.

In our set-up, however small the congregation might be, almost every one is given some kind of responsibility. For every ten members, there is a deacon or a deaconess. Besides we have youth leaders, directors of evangelistic outreach, Sunday School teachers and superintendents, and so on.

Our program of Theological Education by Extension arouses interest in the minds of the lay people. They study the Word of God and go out to evangelize and to witness.

The church is not an end in itself, it is only a means to an end. Our main concern is to plant churches which in turn will produce more churches, thus fulfilling the dual role of a sodality and modality. As already indicated in Chapter VII, most of our churches were planted through direct laymen participation in evangelism.

Lay activity during the year culminates during an annual event known as the National Missionary Congress, held on January 26, (Republic Day) of every year. The meeting is well attended by over 1,000 people. This is a great opportunity for us to inform the people of what is happening throghout Madras City and thereby take all the congregations with us in achieving the objective. A graphic account of church growth to date is given, themes and challenges are displayed through diagrams and charts.

5. Pastors' Monthly Conferences and prayer Meetings.

One of the great advantages in city evangelism, is the opportunity workers have to get to meet each other often to discuss and share things with each other.

Every second Monday evening of the month we have a pastors' prayer meeting in some pastor's home. This begins with fellowship and tea. During the last Monday of every month, we have our worker's conference at OMS-ECI Head-quarters.

Besides the reading of monthly reports from every church and having discussions on them, we take time to systematically study books on evangelism, conversions, and church growth. Through group study we come to understand how and when people movements occur and churches grow. We are always alert and eager to learn. We keep ourselves open for new methods and suggestions.

6. House Churches

I do not want my readers to get the impression that long before we launched out on a church planting ministry we had very good working academic knowledge on church growth principles. These strategies and methods evolved in our sincere attempt to evangelize and plant churches.

For instance to establish " House Churches " was not at first our plan or ideal. House Churches arose as a natural solution to a new group of believers looking around for a place to worship and to carry on their business of reaching the yet unreached.

Our churches were born and grew in homes, rented shop buildings, school verandahs, under trees and in the open air. In short, wherever people felt free to come. A house is an ideal place to *begin* a church but not for the continuation of it. I shall discuss the reasons for this in my next chapter.

7. Absence of " Social Gospel "

The well known school and hospital approach of evangelism might have been successful at one time in India. But not any longer. In fact, they have become a great hindrance to the Gospel.

With the link that the ECI has with a foreign missionary society, we might be able to raise funds for orphanages, medical and other social activities. But we have no intentions of getting involved in such things. If at all we do any social service in future we might do it in a limited way.

157

We are very clear in our policy not to get ourselves tied up in any shape or form, with philanthropic activities, For we believe " service mission " is detrimental to the cause of producing strong, self-supporting churches. The young converts who get into the habit of receiving aid may never learn to give. We will not be producing New Testament Churches. Hence there is no place for social gospel in our movement.

8. Keeping the Foreign Missionaries in the Background

These are days for nationalism in India. We are fighting shy of colonialism. A strong feeling against the white man is there. Though this may not be true in villages, people do not want to have anything to do with the white man's religion. I have already indicated a few of the cases of antagonism against missionaries. Perhaps this is the situation all over the world in these days of crossroads in missions.

The activities of the missionaries are confined to teaching in the seminary and strengthening of believers in the churches. The missionary never enters a pioneer area. Even if by chance an American has to drive a vehicle carrying the laymen or students to an area, he leaves them at the outskirts of the town. As far as possible, we keep the Americans out of the scene.

At the same time in some rural areas, Whitemen are still welcomed. People love to talk to a whiteman. Of all the missionaries we have had, Graham and Carol Houghton are the ones who have made a real effort to learn the language of the masses. We admire them for this. The villagers enjoy conversing with them.

9. Conversions with Minimum, Social Dislocation

Defining " people movement, " Dr. McGavran says :
A people movement results from the joint
decision of a number of individuals—whether
five or fivehundred—all from the same people,
which enables them to become Christians without social dislocation while remaining in full
contact with their non–Christian relatives.
(1970 : 297)

Dr. Kraft in his article on "Christian or Cultural Conversion in Practical Anthropology" (1963 : 182–183) brings out that to become a Christian, it is not necessary to pursue a particular philosophy or world view. To become a Christian is not to embrace Western culture. Such attitudes provide a primary hindrance to effective cross-cultural communication to the Christian message. Jesus Christ interacts with man through His word in any culture as His vehicle.

Conversions and people movements, in our ministry, take place with minimum social dislocation. People are not asked to give up their caste and family unit. Some of the traditional customs have been given functional substitutes. For example, there is a custom among Harijans to have a big ceremony on the nineth month of a woman's first pregnancy. This practice has been replaced by a thanksgiving ceremony.

10. Strategizing Web Movements

In the ministry of our Lord and of St. Paul, we find they strategized through certain individuals to bring in families and groups of families. This is called a strategy of web movements. We constantly teach converts to *bring the rest of the family*. We hesitate to baptize individuals immediately after conversion. We encourage them to bring the rest of the family. If that is not possible, we baptize such individuals and then hope for the best.

As a result of this "family unit" policy, hundreds have been brought to the Christian fold. This makes converts feel quite at home. They are joining their own people. Family movements help them to stand together.

11. A Clear Strategy—A Specific Goal

The greatest tragedy in the Christian ministry today is an attitude of taking things for granted. There is no hard, bold plan

to disimple the people of India. There is so much " beating
around the bush." One of the causes for the rapid growth of
the ECI, If I may say so, is a clear cut strategy and a specific goal.

In 1974, we are working with all urgency for our specific
goal which is to have one hundred churches by 1980. This goal
keeps us on course It directs us to our own long-range objective.
Perhaps most of all, it keeps us faithful to God's commission to
call our neighbors and friends to accept abundant and eternal life
through faith in Jesus Christ.

CHAPTER X—PROPOSALS AND RECOMMENDATIONS

Part I—An Urban Strategy

The fact that about 2,500 men and women were discipled and thirty or more churches planted among a few most responsive communities during the last twenty years, though not a spectacular result, shows that the possibilities for evangelizing modern India are enormous. Though the situation might differ from city to city, from north to south, if we systematically declare the good news and strategically from small cells among receptive peoples, we may reasonably expect substantial church growth.

In this part of the chapter, I discuss the following principles and methods that may be applied for church planting ministry in urban situations outside of Madras. In Part II, I shall make some general observations for an overall strategy to disciple the receptive population of India.

A. SIGNIFICANT FACTORS IN URBAN CHURCH PLANTING

1. Conditions Favorable to Church Growth

" Uprooted and transplanted immigrants starting life anew in strange surroundings and needing community and friendship flood into cities." (McGavran 1970 : 282) In Chapter VIII, I have shown how certain immigrants to Madras accepted Christ after arriving in the city, who might not have made a decision for Christ had they remained back in their own villages. There is such openness among some of the newcomers to the city because of the freedom they have from the control of their families. Due to urbanization, there is also a serious erosion of animist belief. City dwellers, to a certain extent, are free from fears and superstitions and other traditional bondages.

One other great advantage in city evangelism is that the people are within reach. We do not have to go on long journeys and walk many miles to find a responsive group in some remote part

161

of the country. That the people of the city live in concentrations, makes it easy for the evangelists to reach them. The three-and four-story apartments built by the Slum Clearanc Board, can easily house two are three Indian villages. This also provides opportunity for young believers of the various congregations to get together and have fellowship with each other and strengthen one another in the Lord. This enables the little congregations to feel a sense of solidarity and unity in purpose and in action.

Moreover, since city Christians live under better economic conditions than the rural and are in the habit of spending money rather than saving it, it becomes possible to bring the city churches more speedily to self-support.

2. Some Barriers to Urban Church Planting

Church planters in urban areas have to counteract some big and small hurdles. First, City evangelism can become discouraging because of population mobility. It is hard to keep track of the people who move from city to city or go back to their native places. Because members constantly move, it becomes very hard, sometimes, to establish a steady congregation. The C^1 members of our churches, wherever they may go are very faithful to the churches and pastors through whom they had found Christ. They continue to send their donations to their "mother churches" and to seek opportunities to establish ECI Churches wherever and whenever they can. We cannot expect the same enthusiasm from C^2 Christians.

The other big barrier to city evangelism is the rapid development of people's total indifference to spiritual matters and the material outlook in life. Attractions and entertainments distract the minds of these sophisticated people. On one hand, this prevents people from putting their trust in Christ. [On the other hand, it makes Christians walk unsteadily and live a double standard.

There is yet another big hurdle in the urban church planting —the cost of land and property. We are constantly up against this in the city of Madras. We have a definite policy not to assist any congragation in buying land before it is officially organized

162

into a church. This, in most cases, takes quite a few years, but by that time the cost of land has risen tremendously, making it impossible to purchase even a small piece of property.

In balance, the favorable conditions for urban church planting outweigh the unfavorable. Great opportunities exist for effective church planting in cities.

B. McGavran-Wagner Recommendations

During the last several years, significant research on urban evangelism has been done on the basis of which Dr. McGavran (1970 : 285–295). Prof. Wagner (1971 : 189–197), and Dr. Greenway (1973 : 204–236) suggest several strategies for urban church planting. Some of their proposals may not apply to urban situations alone. Others could be applied to any responsive community, whether rural or urban. Since I have already expressed the opinion that the urban mind in a broad sense is a phenomenon today not only in cities but also in the villages, I can say that these principles might be put into operation in any part of modern India. I am giving here those strategies suggested by these eminent missiologists, with slight adaptation to make them fit Madras City which I know so well. I also add a summary of the OMS policies for church planting which I call " The Madras Plan. "

1. Communicate Intense Belief in Christ

If cities were strategic points for the spreading of the Gospel in the first century it was also the cities which persecuted the early Christians. Christ was born in a village but crucified in a city— and He continues to be crucified there today. But at the same time, it was in a city when men of different cultures and languages gathered together in one accord. They were all filled with the Holy Spirit and intense belief in Christ. Only then did they carry the Gospel the length and breadth of the Mediterranean World.

2. Discover the Areas of Fertile Soil

One part of the city differs from the other. No one would attempt to evangelize the busy, crowded old city of Calcutta. The chances are among the depressed class of people who are migrating to the newly developing areas.

3. Begin with House Churches

It is very important that when a group of men and women respond to the Gospel we immediately gather them and from them into worshipping and learning cells. Renting a house is the only answer, not only to assure a meeting place for the new group of believers, but also to house the evangelist and his family.

But even house churches face some practical problems. Sometimes the rent is too high or else the house is located where Harijans may not be allowed to enter. The house might belong to an enemy of the enquirer. In many cases, the owner simply refuses to let a house for worship. In other cases, even if the landlord allows it for worship, the house may not be conducive to it. However, despite the disadvantages, the best alternative is to rent a house wherever possible and provide a meeting place until the congregation gets on to its feet. House churches, however, are a temporary expedient. They cannot become permanent places of worship.

4. Prepare to Sacrifice

Planting new churches in cities will cost time and money. We need the right type of Christians and money enough to stabilize the work in every possible way. Every effort must be made to establish permanent and stable churches in cities which can become the "base churches" for countrywide church planting operations. Urban church planting will also require complete identification with the people to whom we share the message of the Gospel.

5. Develop Unpaid Lay Leaders.

As there are more literate persons in the cities, it is relatively easy to train lay leaders among the city Christians. This does not mean to say that the illiterates are unfit to be lay leaders. But Lay people can be better used in cities where the churches may be located close to each other.

164

6. Recognize Persistent Homogeneous Units.

Unlike rural areas, the city is composed of hundreds of homogeneous units. The city also has a considerable cosmopolitan population. But it is for the evangelists to discern which community is responsive and which one is resistant to the Gospel.

7. Multiply Tribe, Caste, and Language Churches.

As I have already pointed out, the immigrants to the city, whether Christian or non-Christian, retain their caste and tribal identities when they come to the cities. It is the prime duty of those who plant churches to be aware of these caste legalities and remember that men like to become Christians without crossing barriers. Churches which arise within ethnic groups grow better than conglomerate churches.

Dr. McGavran has observed four main types of churches in India. They are Syrian Community Church, Tribal Churches, Caste Churches, and Conglomerate Churches. Nevertheless, these general types of churches take different facets as the Christians move to the cities and reorganize themselves. Mr. George Samuel (1972·26-30) who has done an extensive research in the Bombay City Churches has found these following types among them.

a. *Monoethnic* — These are congregations belonging to a single ethnic group. Each congregation is homogeneous in nature because of the particular ethnic group and the language.

b. *Syrian-Monoethnic* — These are congregations of the Syrian Christian background. Though a very small minority cannot identify as " Syrians," still this type of congregation and homogeneous in nature because they all speak Malayalam.

c. *Multiethnie-Fusion* — Members of this types of congregation cannot identify their ethnic origin (or they have forgotten) because of intense intermingling of converts to Christianity in the previous generations.

d. *Preponderant-ethnic* — These are congregations with people belonging to different ethnic groups, but the majority of members belong to one ethnic group. We may call them partially conglomerate churches. The linguistic and denominational affiliations in type "a" churches resulted in formation of most these type of churches.

e. *Syrian - Multiethnic* — The Christians who originally belonged to Syrian background but joined churches from other ethnic groups and made churches of a new and different type.

f. *Multiethnic or Conglomerate* — This a high, elite church of English-speaking Indian Christians of various backgrounds.

h. *English International* — The members of this type of congregation foreigners lifie.

People are created different from each other. They belong to different races, castes and speak different langnages. In an urban strategy, we must help many types of churches to develop their own way of congregating and worshipping the Lord. Each of the above mentioned types can strive to bring to Christ and to to His Church the non-Christians who might feel at home in its congregation.

8. Provide the Theological Base for an Egalitarian Society

We have to plant churches within many cultural and linguistic groups. The churches must be models of the Kingdom of God on earth which, from a biblical standpoint, fight for an egalitarian society.

It is no concidence that communism was born in the "Christian world." Communism arose in answer to failure on the part of the Church and Christianity in applying the biblical teaching on an egalitarian society. It was Christianity that brought the sense of equality in India by lifting up the depressed classes. Even K. M. Panikker (1963 : 50) bears witness to the fact that the original source for the movement of the uplift of the untouchables was the preaching of the Christian missionary. It is the duty of church planters to throw in their lot with the masses and disciple them. Middle class churches, though they do all

166

kinds of social work, are completely cut off from the masses. The Church at present has no answer to the problems of the depressed class of people. Churches must somehow do something to identify with common people.

9. Try "The Madras Plan"

The "Madras Plan" in carrying out that which (OMS) have developed by our experience and convictions about church growth may be summarized as follows :

—Choose any sizeable section of society which you feel is *not resistent* to the Gospel.

—If the area is too big, it may have to be divided into two or more sections to be handled one by one.

—Have ten weeks of systamatic distribution of leaflets, in series, in a chosen area, accompanied by much personal work, street preaching, children's meetings, etc. Weekends are the best time for this kind of program.

—Have a two-week compaign at the close of the ten weeks with public meetings in a suitable place.

—If a handful of people accept Christ or show continued interest, immediately form them into a little cell. Do not hand them over to any carless church people who would not know what to do with new Christians. Planting churches is the birthright of every Christian. Where two or three are gathered together in the name of Christ, He is there in their midst — that is your church.

—Baptize the young converts soon.

—Continue teaching the young believers to be effective witnesses for Jesus Christ, encouraging them to witness soon.

—If you have found the soil to be unproductive, give it one more trial for one other term of twelve weeks and if there has been no tangible evidence of conversions do not hesitate to shift your actives to some responsive area.

Part II—Strategy for India

I shall in this section of the chapter analyze briefly the methods of approach which may be adopted in discipling peoples of India. I shall also recommend certain proposals to multiply churches among the responsive population in this generation.

A. An Honest Appraisal of Church and Mission in India

Just a look at the history of missions in India would tell us the hosts of missionary organizations like the Baptists, CMS, SPA, LMS, Church of Scotland, American Baptists, American Arcot Mission and numerous others have done a significant work for the cause of Christ and His Kingdom. The modern missionary era in the history of the Chrissian Church began in India with William Carey. Scores of thousands of missionaries followed him.

We praise God for being mindful of us. We are greateful to Him for sending hundreds and thousands of His servants from St. Thomas down. We rejoice in Him for fourteen million people who identify themselves as Christians.

Figure 10 in opposite could be an eye opener for the pessimists, and prophets of defeatism in the Christian circles who are of the opinion that the Indian Church is not growing and that the days of missionary enterprise are over. It is heartening to realize that the Christians have multiplied much faster than any other religious group during the last ten years. The Christian population in 1891 was only 1·5 million. In 1971 it has shot up to 14·2 million—a 966% growth !

But wait a minute. Let us not get carried away. Study figure 11. There is still a long way for Christians to catch up with the so called " majority " Community. If the Christians grow at this rate it will take more than 100 years to outgrow the non-Christians. But that is only if the rest of the population determined not to grow any more ! In fact they are growing at an average rate of 25 percent each decade.

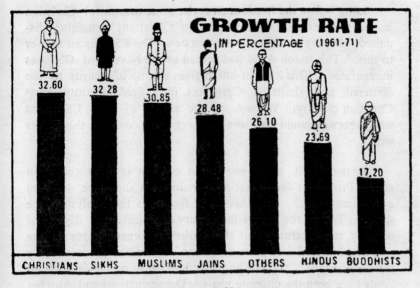

FIG. 10.

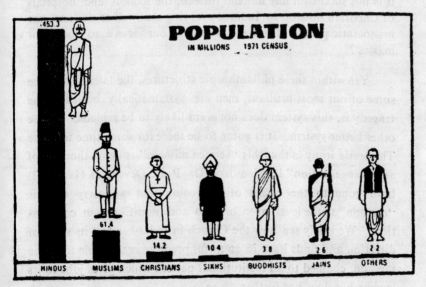

FIG. 11.

169

Long before the freedom struggle, some thoughtful Christian leaders were aware of the dangers in Christians remaining disunited, carrying on the sectarian quarrels. The CSI was an answer to this. This union trend had spread to the North and CNI was inaugurated. This kind of union gives a sense of security to the scattered and shattered Christians in a predominantly non-Christian country. We welcome the efforts of these Christians who otherwise could not have anything else to occupy themselves with.

Be that as it may, our main concern is what the main stream Protestant denominations are doing in any shape or form evangelize India ? The answer is found in the analysis of the structure left by the parent missionary organizations. Rightly or wrongly, the structure of all the missionary organizations in the past one hundred fifty years or so has been one of predominantly service missions. Schools and hospitals and orphanages of all kinds have been the ultimate goals. Denominations and churches of every description did some evangelism and church planting, but greatly stressed service. This "school and hospital approach" might have been successful in certain areas in the early days, but it is not successful any more. Instead, the schools and hospitals of Christian mission in India are serving the well-to-do and the aristocratic people of India. Where is our service to the poor masses ?

Yet within these philanthropic structures, the talents of some some of our most brilliant men are systamatically buried. The tragedy is, this system does not seem likely to be replaced by ane other better system. It is going to be there for some time to come The crude irony is that this "service mission" is being thought of as "evangelization" ! Men like Dr. P. D. Devandan (1959 : 62) have gone to the extent of proposing that we carry on this "mission" to the level of "Christian and non-Christian cooperation." We easily see how the Church in India has lost its sense of direction and finds itself in an awful predicament, unable to define mission, chained to an institutional pattern which gives jobs to its leaders but does not further cause.

170

While on the other hand, there were hundreds of servants of Christ, both foreign and national from the times of De Nobili to Reymond Panikar of our time, who with great success tried to understand and interpret the Indian philosophy in the light of the message of the Gospel. India is not going to see another E. Stanley Jones who had such a remarkable ministry among the educated classes of India. The impact he made on the life of Mahatma Gandhi and thousands of other non-Christians through his lectures and book is very astonishing and striking indeed. Our only disappointment is that men like Dr. Stanley Jones have not left any structure for the future of a similar ministry among the educated classes of India. Many seekers have come and gone through his Ashrams; but it is very distressing to see that we are not able to identify any of his followers or their little cells in any of the cities and towns.

A question may be asked, was there any possibility of planting churches among the high castes at all ? The answer is probably "no." Only the lower castes in India really responded and Christ lifted them up and made them high "caste". Whenever the missions identified themselves with the masses, there were conversions. A major breakthrough among the masses of India is yet to take place.

B. Stumbling Blocks or Stepping Stones

Several forces at work in India today need to be counteracted with the gospel message. From one angle, if we look at them, they might appear as great barriers to the Gospel, but if we approach them from another angle, the same stumbling blocks can be turned into stepping stones.

1. People's Capacity for Religion

Indians at large have a great capacity for belief and religion. They are prepared to believe anything and everything. This is where. perhaps, the great danger lies and this is where a non-Christian begins. Christ has already been accepted in India as one of the gods. While this is not what we want that should happen, it is how sometimes the " leavening " takes place.

171

There is a real danger on our part not to recognize the inherent values God has already placed in their hearts—a capacity to believe things. It is also equally dangerous to recognize these values in paganism to the extent of minimizing the uniqueness of Christ and Christianity and thus falling into syncretism or relativism.

After a Hindu has already given a place for Christ, it is our duty to continue to persuade the man to accept Christ as the Lord, the only Avatar, and the only Saviour of mankind.

2. Secularism

There is no real danger with secularism in India. As a matter of fact, it is nothing but a great surprise and the providence of God that India is today a secular and democratic country. This secularism can very well be traced in large part to Christian teaching. This being the case, the Christian in India doesn't reject secularism as something entirely ungodly but helps formulate a theology out of it, based on Scripture of what I would like to call " theosecularism."

The duty of the Christian is to baptize every system into Christ for " according to God's good pleasure which He hath purposed in Himself ; that in the fulness of time He might gather in one all thing in Christ both which are in heaven, and which are on earth. " (Eph. 1 : 9–10) The fulness of time for India has come and secularism which helps to break away traditional beliefs, is one sign of it. Secularism is not a march backward but forward. Chirst is a symbol of progress and he is already in it with his presence.

3. The Caste

Is caste stumbling block or else a stepping stone ? Can caste be used for the propagation of the Gospel ?

There is a good side and a bad side to caste. It is the prime duty of the Christian to know both sides of it. Let us first look at the apparently good side of caste. For centuries the missionaries could not properly understand the caste system. Let me

172

narrate here an embarrassing situation in which a young missionary was placed over this issue.

Early in 1963, in one of the summer camps at the Sat Tal Ashram of Dr. E. Stanley Jones in India, they had a seminar on " Caste and Christianity." In one of the sessions, a certain young missionary gave his talk on the subject. He vehemently attacked the caste system in India and went on to condemn the Indian Christians among whom the caste feelings were much prevalent. He further suggested that at least the Christians must set an example in mixing with other caste Christians through intermarriages and other possible union. The missionary thought that he had really delivered his goods. But, during question hour the first question came from the floor from one gentleman whose name, incidently, was Brave. Mr. Brave wanted to know which country the missionary came from and how many children he had. The missionary replied politely that he came from the U.S.A., and that he had three daughters. Then Mr. Brave came out with a most personal and trying question when he asked the missionary " Will you let your daughters marry black youth in your country ?" The missionary fumpled along and finally came out with " I don't know what I would do under those circumstances." Mr. Brave replied kindly, " We know what you would do ; you would never allow your daughters to marry Negroes—not necessarily because of your racial prejudice—you may even love the Negroes, but you wouldn't encourage mixed marriages for certain social and cultural reasons." He went on to say, " You are not the first missionary who has picked on us. Please try to have a sympathetic understanding of the caste situation in this country."

On the one hand this caste system may be compared to the class or racial institutions found among other societies. But by its own merits or demerits, there is nothing parallel to caste in any other society anywhere else in the world. (Hutton 1963 : 46) There were some missionaries who have made correct judgment on the caste situatton. Mr. Grant makes this valuable observation :

In the West, caste is commonly misunderstood and undervalued. First-hand contact inspires considerable respect for the values inherent in caste. The caste serves in many ways as a brotherhood, exercising a moral discipline among its members and providing economic support for those who are in need. It offers the security that goes with a sense of belonging. It gives many of the satisfactions that North Americans seek by joining fraternal orders or service clubs. Exclusion from his caste is the worst disaster that can befall an Indian for it robs him not only of his material security, but also moral sanctions that mold him into accepted patterns of social living. The sudden disintegration of the caste system would probably result in moral chaos, for an Indian is not accustomed to making decisions as a self-contained individual. (Grant 1959 : 9-10)

Rev. J. W. Grant points out very clearly the tragic state of an individual when he is " suddenly " detached for his particular caste and community. This is something the church planters in India must constantly bear in mind.

I would partly agree with Rev. Canjanan Gamaliel (1967 : 100) who thinks that caste is the " divine order of preservation in society in India until the Gospel can transform society and create new order of preservation." But I hesitate to call caste wholly and solely a *divine* order. There is too much evil in it. Though untouchability has been made illegal, it is very prevalent in villages even to this day. Yet I would like to say that caste is a necessary evil for the function of society in India. I prefer to think that man made it. It is part of culture. Man made it and man can change it and is changing it. People movements and web movements could be well organized within caste. Caste helps a society to make collective decisions. So let us learn to accept this " order " than declare a war against it.

4. Syncretism.

Syncretism is a commonly accepted philosphy of life among most of the Hindus. Even an average Hindu would say that all religions are one and we are all going to the same place just as the rivers that flow from different sources finally get to the same ocean. It is hard to convince a Hindu of the supremacy of Christ and Christianity.

The Hindus have now gone a step further and have taken the offensive. Dr. Radhakrishnan, who is hailed as the saviour of Hinduism, with his extraordinary knowledge of Christian thought and philosophy makes plain to Christians and Hindus alike the superiority of Hinduism as a way of life, characterized as it is by that width of outlook which makes it so much better fitted to be universal religion than Christianity with its narrowness, its dogmas, and its " intolerance ". He calls his religion as *"Sanatanadharma"* (the eternal religion). Dr. Radhakrishnan, as a typical Brahmin, with all his "cleverness", does not realize that he is trying to hatch an egg much bigger than he is. We could understand that he is attempting to redefiine Hinduism which has been dubbed as a " pagan " and " primitive " religion with all the numerous gods and the " evil " system of caste. We would like to pose a question to the eminent scholar philosopher and former President of India, what has he got in his philosophical system that is going to ultimately relieve the sufferings of the depressed community in India? Who cares for his " Sanatana Dharma " ? People are looking for something—anything—which can liberate them from the four thousand year-old Brahmin suppression.

Bishop Stephen Neil (1971 : 571) commenting on Dr. Radhakrishnan's neo-Hinduism says.

> It is unlikely that these threats will grow any less between now and the end of the centuary. It is probable that the churches will find the world situation increasingly unfavorable to them. In this, there is no special reason for discouragement. The Church has often been here before, and has made difficulty the stepping stone to recovery.

I see here a key thought for the successs of Christian religion in India. The future of mission in India lies in our ability to make the most stumbling blocks as stepping stones.

With this brief sketch on the present state of affairs, of the various forces that are at work in India, I go on to make these following proposals a conclusion to my book.

C. The Ten-Point Proposals.

These ten-point proposals might become the tools to disciple the responsive population of India.

1. Let the Church in India be a " Waiting " Church.

By that I mean a church that is waiting on God for an out-pouring of the Holy Spirit. A great spiritual awakening among the Christians can result in passion for souls and making sacrific for the cause of evangelizm in India.

2. Go, Preach, Disciple, Teach.

With this fourfold ideal strategy, we not only go to the people and preach to them, but when they put their trust in Christ we disciple them by baptizing them in the name of the Father, the Son, and the Holy Spirit. Then we continue to teach them to grow into perfection. Discipling and teaching should not be confused with each other. Teaching is a follow-up of discipling.

3. Focus on the Common people, Even on the Depressed Classes

Much of the energies of the evangelizing agencies are dissipa-ted by not focusing on the responsive. " Win the winnable while they are winnable ", say Dr. McGavran. The Harijans and the other depressed castes of India, on the most sober estimate, are the responsive communities in India. No time must be lost in multiplying churches among these people.

4. Make Conversions Within the Social Structure.

People need not be asked to change their social customs and other traditional behaviors. To become a Christian does not mean to wear pants and coats. Men and women may be asked to follow Christ still being proud of their culture or caste to which they belong. So let us strive to make conversion with minimum social dislocation.

5. Christ Must Increase, Christianity Must Decrease.

I am not saying that Christianity must be done away with. I am only saying that a Christianity which is closely identified with the West must be eventually shipped back to were it came from. When Christ is " lifted up " as the liberator of India, as already been as He is going to attract He millions of people to Himslf. This I can give in writing in my own blood. Christ must be proclaimed as the God of our salvation and as liberator from social, political, and economic depression. Cells of Christians must be formed. The Indian Church must be formed in its own biblical molds.

6. Plant Churches That Plant Churches

Church is not an end in itself, it is only a means to an end. The Church is a missionary community. Wherever this principle has been applied, the newly organized churches produced daughter churches rapidly. Our ultimate aim must be to plant chunches which in turn would plant churches and on and on without end. This could be brought about only through a lay movement. Therefore, it is impediment to keep hammer along at the priest-hood of all believers.

7. Strategize People Movements

People in India are not just individuals. There is the extended family and the clan and the caste. The street corner preachings and bazar preachings and the handing out of tracts, to the passers by may bring in few stray individuals to the Christian fold. But the most effective and succesful way to evangelize is through the families and caste groups who are responsive to the Gospel. Mobilize the Christians to bring their relatives to Christ. Our slogan must be " Families for Christ " and " Relatives for Christ."

8. Minimize " Service Missions "

We are not saying that the social gospel must be completely done away with. We only say let these things be done in proportion. Let not priority be given for " service mission." One of the causes for success in the " Madras pattern " was absence of social service activities.

177

9. Restructure Seminaries

Seminaries should not be centers of more academic pursuit, but they must be idea factories which produce men of action with missionary zeal and vision. If a student has not gained practical knowledge in discipling non-Christians and strived to become an active church planter while in the seminary, he is not going to learn it out in the field. To our knowledge, church planting ministry has been carried out by two of the seminaries in Latin America. (Greenway 1970 : 152)

Seminaries in India also should open out-stations to carry out theological education be extension programs.

10. Indigenity in Theology, Worship, and Mission

Much has been said about the need of indigenous theology and worship these days, but no one seems to be concerned for an indigenous mission. This is very important in these days when national feelings are so high. We must constantly expose ourselves to new national methods to reach the nationals.

The one I think would be effective along this line is a " *Padayatra* " (foot pilgrimage), which I myself feel burdened to carry out in a few years when the situation ripens. I may begin from Cape Comerin and walk five or ten miles a day, visiting village after village proclaiming the " good news " and establishing churches on the way and finally reach Madras.

I am sure there must be still better Indian methods through which the people of India may be discipled. We have to constantly keep ourselves open to the leading of the Holy Spirit to show us new strategies by which an effective church planting ministry may be set in motion. The furture of mission in India depends upon our ability to use indigenous methods to disciple the population of our beloved land.

BIBLIOGRAPHY

ALISON, Henry Allen, Jr.
>   1961   *Introduction to Descriptive Linguistic.* Holt, Reinhart, Winson.

ALLEN, Roland
>   1930   *Missonary Methods : St. Paul's or Ours.* London, World Dominion Press.

ANDERSON, Nels
>   1964   *Urbanism and Urbanization.* Leiden, E. J. Brill.

BARNET, H. G.
>   1953   *Innovation : The Basis of Culture Change.* New York, McGraw-Hill Book Company.

BERGEL, Egon Ernest
>   1955   *Urban Sociology.* McGraw-Hill Book Company, Inc.

BESSEY, C. E.
>   1915   *University Studies of the University of Nebraska.* Vol. 15. Lincoln, University of Nebraska Press.

BRANDENFELS, Fred
>   1963   "Some Sociological Factors in Group Conversion to Christianity." An unpublished thesis, Hartford Seminary Foundation.

BRAUN, Neil
>   1971   *Laity Mobilized.* Grand Rapids, William B. Eerdmans Publishing Company.

BREEZE, Gerald
>   1966   *Urbaniztion in Newly Developing Countries.* Bureau of Urban Research, Princeton, Princeton University.

BULSARA, Jal F.
>   1964   *Problems of Rapid Urbanization in India.*

CENSUS OF INDIA

1911

1971   Manager of Publication, New Delhi.

CORNELIUS, Collapalli

1971   "Urban Church Growth Among Telugu Baptist Church in South India." An unpublished thesis, School of World Mission, Fuller Theological Seminary, Pasadena, Calif.

COWMAN, Lettie B

1967   *Charles E. Cowman : Missionary-Warrior.* Grand Rapids, Zondervan Publishing House.

COX, Harvey

1967   *The Secular City.* New York, Macmillan Company.

DAVIS, Roy

1973   Letter to author, March 6.

DEVANANDAN, P. D.

1959   *The Gospel and Renascent Hinduism.* London, SCM Press Ltd.

DUEWEL, Wesley

1970   "The Spirit's Ministry Through OMS." Unpublished report for OMS International.

ERNY, Engenn

1950   "India's Open Door," *Missionary Standard*, June.

FIRTH, C. B.

1961   *An Introduction to Indian Church History.* The Senate of Serampere College, The Christian Literature Society.

GAMALIEL, Jamrs Canjanan

1967   "The Church in Kerala." An unpublished thesis, School World Mission, Fuller Theological Seminary, Pasadena, California.

GNANADOSS, V. S. D.

1972   Letter to author, November 20.

GNANARAJ, N. J.
1972 Letter to author, November.

GOLWALKAR, W. S.
1966 *Bunch of Thoughts.* Bangalore Press.

GRANT, John Webster
1959 *God's People in India.* Toronto, The Ryerson Press.

GREENWAY, Roger S.
1973 *An Urban Strategy for Latin America.* Grand Rapids,
Baker Book Home.

GREENWAY, Roger S.
1970 "A Church Planting Method That Works in Urban
Areas," Evangelical Miasion Quarterly, Spring, 1970.

HASTINGS, James, ed.
1935 "The Dravidian," London, England, *Encyclopedia of
Religion and Ethics,* Vol 5.

HUTTON, J. H.
1963 *Caste in India.* Oxford University Press.

IRCHIK, Eugene F.
1969 *Politics and Social Conflict in South India.*

JONES, E. Stanley
1859 *Conversion.* Nashville, Abingdon Press.

JOSEPH, I.
1966 Interview with author, 1966.

JOSEPH, Victor
1972 Letter to author, November 13.

KANTHIAH PILLAI, N. C.
1939 "Thamilar Charithiram," *History of the Tamils.*
Thiyagarayanagar, Madras.

KILBOURNE, E. L.
1940 Travel letter, March.

KRAFT, Charles H.
1963 "Christian or Cultural Conversion," *Practical Anthro
pology,* July-Aug., 1963.

LAHOVARY, N.
1962 *Dravidian Origins and the West Orient Longman.*
Bombay, Calcutta, Madras, New Delhi.

LATOURETTE, Kenneth Scott
 1953 *History of Christianity.* New York, Harper and Row.

LEVAI, Blaise
 1972 *Ask An Indian About India.* New York, Friendship Press.

 1957 *Revolutions in Missions.* Calcutta, YMCA Publishing House.

MANUAL OF THE EVANGELICAL CHURCH OF INDIA
 1972

McGAVRAN, Donald A., ed.
 1955 *Bridges of God.* New York, Friendship Press.

 1962 *Church Growth and Group Conversion.* Lucknow, The Lucknow Publishing House.

 1970 *Understanding Church Growth.* Grand Rapids, William B. Eerdmans Publishing Company.

MORAES, George Mark
 1964 *A History of Christianity From the Early Time of St. Thomas to St. Xaviour.* AD 52–1542, Bombay.

MULLER, Max F.
 1909 *Sacred Books of the East.* Vol. 25, 45. Oxford at Cleredon Press.

NEIL, Stephen
 1971 *A History of Christian Missions.* Peilcan History of the Church : 6. Penguin Books.

NELSON. Amirtharaj
 1973 " Madras City Churches." An unpublished thesis, Scool of World Mission, Fuller Theological Seminary, Pasadena, California.

ORR, Edwin J,
 1970 *Evangelical Awakening in India.* New Delhi, Mashihi Sahatya Samsta.

PANIKAR, K. M.
 1963 *The Foundatians of New India.* London, George F. Unwin Ltd.

PEARSON, B, H.
 1967 *Men+God.* Men for Mission International, Greenwood, Indiana.

PARAMASIVANANDAM, A, M.
> 1960 *Tamilnadu Through Ages.* (In Tamil) Tamil Kalai Illam, Madras.

PHILLIPPE, Elma
> 1953 " Madras Bible Seminary Opened, *" Missionary Standard,* October.

PHILLIPPE, Garnet G.
> 1972 Letter to author, November 10.

PICKET, Washam J.
> 1933 *Chris:ian Mass Movements in India.* Lucknow, Lucknow Publishing House.

RABE, Rudolf M.
> 1960 " The Call of the City. *"Missionary Standard,* November.

RAM, J.
> 1969 *Hindi Against India.* New Delhi, Hind Publishers.

RAMANUJAM, K. S.
> 1971 " Challenge and Response." An intimate report on Tamilnadu Politics (1967–71), Hindustan Times.

RIGBY, David J.
> 1955 " Evangelism in Madars Area," *Missionary Standard,* June,

RIGBY, David J,
> 1255 " The Onward March in Madras," *The Missionary Standard,* July.
> 1972 " Early Days of OMS Ministry in Madras." Correspondence written for author.

SADHUSINGH, P. J.
> 1973 Letter to author, March 20.

SAMUEL, George J.
> 1972 " Church Growth Strategy in Terms of Urbanization in India." Paper submitted as part requirement for course, Frontiers in Missionary Strategy, School of World Mission, Fuller Theological Seminary, Pasadena, California.

SARGANT, N. C.
> *The Dispersian of the Tamil Church.* I.S.P.C.K.

SARGUNAM, M. Ezra
    1972 "Church Planting." *Light of Life*, October.

SJOBERG, Andre F.
    1971 *Symposium on Dravidian Civilization.* New York, Jenkins Publishing Company.

SMITH, Ceorge (1933–1912)
    n. c. *The Conversion of India.* New York, Fleming H. Revell Co.

THURSTON, E, (assisted by RANGACHARI)
    1908 *Castes and Tribes of Southern India.* Vol. IV, VII, Madras.

TIPPETT, A. R.
    1967 *Solomon Islands Christianity.* London, Lutherworth Press.

TRACT SERIES 4, 5
    1970 "Manam Mara Vali Vounda" (Is There a Way for Changed Life ?) Evangelical Church of India, 5, Waddell Road, Kilpauk, Madras.

WAGNER, Peter C.
    1971 *Frontiers in Missionary Strategy.* Chicago, Moody Press.

WINTER, Ralph
    1971 "Churches Need Missions Because Modalities Need Sodalities," *Evangelical Mission Quarterly,* Summer, 1971.

WOYTINSKY, W. S.
    1969 *India the Awakening Giant.* New York, Harper and Brothers.

ZACHARIA, K. C. & BOGUE, DONALD, J.
    1962 Urbanization and Migration in India, Berkley. University of California Press.

ZINKIN, JAYA
    1962 Caste Today. London Institute of Race Relations, Oxford University Press.